GETTING IT DONE

THE TRANSFORMING POWER OF SELF-DISCIPLINE

ANDREW J. DuBRIN, Ph.D.

PETERSON'S/PACESETTER BOOKS
PRINCETON, NEW JERSEY

To Clare,
the second of the new generation

Getting It Done is published by Peterson's/Pacesetter Books.

Pacesetter Books is a trademark of Peterson's Guides, Inc.

Cover Illustration by Sandra Filippucci

Interior Design by Kathy Kikkert

Library of Congress Cataloging-in-Publication Data

DuBrin, Andrew J.
    Getting it done : the transformational power of self-discipline /
Andrew J. DuBrin.
        p.   cm.
    Includes bibliographical references (p. 223) and index.
    ISBN 1-56079-470-4
    1. Self-control. 2. Success. I. Title.
BF632.D73   1995
153.8—dc20   94-42263
                                                                   CIP

Printed in the United States of America
10 9 8 7 6 5 4 3 2

CONTENTS

Have you ever sat back and pondered such questions as:

- How can I become more successful and happy?
- Isn't there a way I can get on track to starting my own business?
- What can I do to improve my golf game?
- What can I do to meet my work deadlines so that my boss values me more?
- How can I make my way out of debt and stop financing purchases?
- Why can't I get my weight down to where I've always wanted it to be?

Do you see the common element they all share? It is the potential for a satisfying result to an action taken. If you have at least average intelligence, talent, motivation, and skills, you *can* achieve many worthwhile goals in life—as long as you also develop self-discipline. By self-discipline I mean the ability to work systematically and progressively toward a goal until it is achieved. And being self-disciplined doesn't preclude having fun in life. A self-disciplined person doesn't lead a life of self-sacrifice, abstention from pleasure, or continuous self-punishment. Instead, she experiences the joy, exhilaration, and contentment that stems from achieving worthwhile goals. While the undisciplined person might achieve a modicum of fleeting pleasures, the self-disciplined person enjoys a harvest of pleasures. Guided by a personal mission, she achieves day-by-day satisfactions from pursuing the mission, and savors personal victories.

Consider this scenario: Two people in the marketing department of a multinational company decide to study Spanish because their company has developed an affiliate in Mexico. Michael dabbles in his study of Spanish but decides to drop the program because the learning project is interfering with his television-watching time. Bernadette keeps at it, studying for a minimum of one hour per day. She too doesn't want to sacrifice television-watching time, so decides to devote at least some time to watching Spanish-language programs. After one year, she doesn't even miss the hour per day invested in study. She begins to take pride in her ability to learn a second language and becomes increasingly confident as her knowledge base increases daily. Michael can't even account for what he did with the hour per day that he saved by not studying another language.

Bernadette's payoff comes two years later (a self-disciplined person is patient for results), when she is promoted to an international marketing position for which she has to make monthly visits to the Mexican affiliate. She got the job because she met the position qualification of "ability to speak and write Spanish." Her self-discipline brought her both a higher-paying, more exciting job, and the satisfaction of personal development. In contrast, Michael put himself out of the running because he couldn't stay focused on the intermediate-range goal of being promoted or the short-range goal of learning Spanish.

I have written *Getting It Done* to help people do what is necessary to achieve worthwhile and complex goals in work and personal life. My experience indicates clearly that all forms of self-help and self-improvement are unattainable without self-discipline. Take for example the millions of people who have attended work habit and time management seminars and have studied books and magazine articles on the same topic. For most of them, within three months after attending the seminar or doing the reading, their desks are a mess. Furthermore, they fall behind schedule, lose important items, and procrastinate as much as ever.

Without the knowledge of how to use self-discipline to achieve what you want, efforts at improved time management—and all other worthwhile goals—will fizzle. To help you harness the transformational power of self-discipline, I approach learning self-discipline from several angles. In Chapter 1, I provide details about the benefits of self-discipline and present a general framework for achieving self-discipline. In Chapter 2, I introduce the concept of sacrificing short-term gratification for long-term delight, emphasizing the importance of taking the long-range view. Chapter 3 presents techniques for overcoming procrastination, the leading negative consequence of lacking self-discipline. In Chapters 4 and 5 you'll learn how to use self-discipline to fully contribute to two of the major thrusts in today's modern workplace—practicing self-leadership and achieving high quality. Chapter 6 explains how you can use self-discipline to be more imaginative and creative.

How self-discipline and self-management can be applied to enhance personal development is discussed in Chapter 7. And in Chapter 8, I show how you can use self-discipline to control such counterproductive habits as alcohol abuse, food abuse, and tobacco abuse. Following along similar lines, in Chapter 9, I describe how you can apply self-discipline to managing stress. In Chapter 10, you'll learn how self-discipline can help you overcome adversity.

Finally, in Chapter 11, I encourage you to use the transformational power of self-discipline to move your life to a higher plane: By using self-discipline to achieve the flow experience—total involvement in the task at hand—you can work toward your maximum capacity and achieve peak performance.

To help guide you through the many suggestions and specific steps for enhancing your self-discipline, you'll find many case examples, checklists, quizzes, and exercises. But keep this in mind: Reading this book is the easy part. You will need to exercise the self-discipline skills learned within these pages to achieve the long-term goals you strive for.

ACKNOWLEDGMENTS

My primary thanks go to Diane Zielinski, a communications professional at the Rochester Institute of Technology. Diane met with me several years ago to suggest that I write a book about self-discipline. Her reasoning was that the lack of self-discipline is a prime contributor to most personal and societal problems. Major thanks also go to my editor, Andrea Pedolsky, for her enthusiastic acceptance of the concept of a book about self-discipline, and for her numerous suggestions for improving the manuscript. I also thank Andrea and my production editor, Bernadette Boylan, for the self-disciplined way in which they moved the book through production.

Two of my former research associates played a major role in creating this book. C. Jason Koerfel conducted an extensive computer search of all the scientific and general-interest information about self-discipline and self-control. Charles Young capitalized on his many valuable contacts in politics and law enforcement to prepare valuable case histories of self-disciplined people.

Thanks also to all my loved ones for helping make the self-disciplined life of a writer even more enjoyable. Specifically I thank Carol Bowman, my significant other, and the DuBrins in closest contact with me: Melanie, Douglas, Drew, Rosie, and Clare.

CHAPTER 1

THE MASTER KEY TO SUCCESS

Becoming successful and happy depends on many inherited and acquired factors. Only the naive would deny the importance of such success factors as intelligence, education, mental and physical energy, imagination, emotionally supportive parents, political skill, and luck. Add to this list dozens of other factors—such as good communication skills, special talents, outstanding role models, computer savvy, great ethics, and great contacts.

The painful reality is that many people have most of the factors just listed in their favor, yet still fall short of reaching their potential. Without self-discipline, you can rarely achieve big success and big happiness. In the sense used here, self-discipline is the ability to work systematically and progressively toward a goal until it has been achieved.[1] Being self-disciplined means staying focused.

Combined with the right talents and skills, self-discipline is your master key to success and happiness. Without an appropriate degree of self-discipline, you run the risk of being a lifelong wannabe. President Theodore Roosevelt summed it up incisively when he said:

> The one quality which sets one [person] apart from another—the key which lifts one to every aspiration while others are caught up in the mire of mediocrity—is not talent, formal education, nor intellectual brightness; it is self-discipline. With self-discipline, all things are possible. Without it, even the simplest goal can seem like the impossible dream.[2]

THE PAYOFF FROM BEING SELF-DISCIPLINED

Since you're holding this book in your hands, I'm sure you have few doubts about the payoff from self-discipline. Still, I think a look at some of the prevailing thoughts and research about the benefits of self-discipline will fire your emotions further and encourage you to develop the habits necessary for achieving it.

Higher Productivity and Quality

An extraordinary benefit of self-discipline is that it facilitates higher productivity and quality. Self-disciplined workers outperform their less disciplined counterparts, and their output reflects higher quality. All other factors being equal, wouldn't most of us prefer that a mechanic with high self-discipline replace our cars' brake linings? Or, having a highly self-disciplined neurosurgeon repair a ruptured artery in our brain.

Novelist and nonfiction writer Michael Crichton exemplifies how self-discipline contributes to productivity and quality. A friend notes that Crichton's favorite line is "butt to chair." When working on a book, Crichton arises at 4:00 a.m. to drive to his office in Santa Monica, California; he returns home at 5:30 p.m. for family activities. While at work, Crichton says, "I might as well have gone away. More and more, I don't particularly want to leave. I have all these ideas. It's a compulsion."[3] I suspect the extraordinary fame and income Crichton derives from his self-disciplined activity contribute immensely to his sense of happiness and well-being.

Self-discipline benefits people competing in many arenas. When Harvard Business School conducted a study to determine the common characteristics of top-performing salespeople, researchers found that most salespeople can be top sellers if they are willing to study, concentrate, and focus on their performance. In addition, they discovered that top producers had

> SELF-DISCIPLINE COMBINED WITH THE RIGHT TALENTS AND SKILLS IS THE MASTER KEY TO SUCCESS AND HAPPINESS.

above-average willpower and determination: No matter how much they felt the temptation to give up, they persisted in pursuit of their goals. Self-discipline was the key success factor.[4]

Garrett Williams was vice president of Quality Training and Management at Atlantic Printing Industries (he recently died from complications during routine surgery). He made these observations about the link between self-discipline and productivity:

> A person with discipline will approach a task with a positive attitude because he or she is comfortable with the challenges that may lie ahead. People shut out opportunities because they perceive them as being difficult or impossible to achieve. There is always a way, and it takes self-discipline to get there.
>
> People who discipline themselves will achieve greater success in everything they do. They will also experience a greater sense of personal satisfaction from getting something extraordinary done. Once you have reaped the rewards of what hard work and

7

discipline can do, you will expect the same from every performance because you know that it's possible. Those who lack self-discipline are only cheating themselves because they can achieve so much more if they realize their capabilities.

Better Performance in School

As most teachers and parents realize, self-discipline leads to better learning and higher grades in school. A major contributor to poor school performance at all educational levels is low self-discipline. An investigation was made of the relationship between several personality factors and grades among 3,200 college men and women. (Note that this study was concerned with personality factors, not intelligence. Personality was measured by a standard test, the California Psychological Inventory.) One of the themes that emerged from the study was that high-potential students score high on self-discipline. In addition, high-potential students think independently and are relatively free from self-aggrandizing motives.[5] These findings imply that self-disciplined people can work well without a strong need of group support. In addition, they are more caught up in the love of the task than impressing others with their greatness.

Research has also shown that self-discipline is a key success factor for medical students. In a survey of 173 medical school faculty about the desirable characteristics of applicants, consensus was reached on three: self-discipline, sensitivity to people, and brightness.[6] The results support the view that self-discipline leads to success, when combined with the right skills and mental ability.

Of course, achieving good grades is not the only benefit of self-discipline. Students who commit themselves to a learning goal, and passionately pursue that goal, achieve a higher skill level than those students simply intent on passing exams. Two germane examples are the acquisition of computer and foreign language skills. Students who have the self-discipline to build their competence and knowledge day by day are much more likely to use their skills upon course completion. In contrast, students who lack commitment to learning computers or a foreign language are less likely to integrate these skills into their life.

A self-disciplined student would typically say, "I'm trying to build skills and acquire knowledge that will improve my life and my career." The less disciplined student is more likely to say, "I need to do well in this course so I can graduate and get a job."

Enhances Reliability

A wonderful consequence of working with self-disciplined people is that they are reliable. The self-disciplined person *does* put your check in the mail, complete a report on time, and finishes remodeling your kitchen in a timely fashion. As a result, the self-disciplined person builds a reputation of credibility and reliability. Customers and company employees love doing business with a reliable person. Self-discipline and reliability are inextricably linked because the self-disciplined person focuses on a deadline and does everything in his power to achieve it.

More Incisive Problem Solving

Another work-related consequence of self-discipline is that it leads to more incisive, thorough problem solving. The self-disciplined person stays focused on a problem until unearthing its root cause. Although such elegant problem solving cannot be achieved in all instances, the self-disciplined mind at least moves in the direction of deeper problem solving. A less disciplined problem solver might grab at a superficial analysis of a problem to save time and mental effort.

An example of self-disciplined thinking in business is the McKinsey Method, named after the problem-solving mode of the professional staff of the management consulting firm, McKinsey & Co. The McKinsey Method is a cool, analytical approach to management that challenges assumptions and rejects wishful thinking. A former McKinsey consultant calls the method "ruthless logic": "You cut through emotions and people's opinions and get down to facts. Discipline has been the foundation for my ability to work through complicated situations."[7] Self-discipline is required because the problem solver stays focused on the goal of probing until the true facts of the problem surface.

Minimization of Daydreaming on the Job

A pleasant reverie on the job offers a few modest advantages. Conjuring your favorite vacation or sex fantasy while in a meeting may relieve the tedium of the moment. Or if you are enmeshed in a stress-elevating moment such as listening to an irate customer, a pleasant daydream can temporarily relieve stress. After a few minutes of relaxation, you might be recharged and able to deal with the pressures of the moment.

Frequent daydreaming on the job, however, offers more negative than positive consequences. Many industrial accidents are directly attributable to daydreaming; accidentally destroyed computer files often have the same origin. The person who daydreams during a meeting has a glazed facial appearance that does not impress the boss. Furthermore, abundant daydreaming leads to substantial losses in productivity.

The highly self-disciplined person gives himself an automatic signal should a drift toward daydreaming begin. Flashing through his mind is the thought, "Get back on track. You're accomplishing nothing." Instead of daydreaming to relieve stress, he might use an on-the-spot relaxer, such as exhaling and inhaling, or consciously relaxing his muscles.

Does all this mean that the self-disciplined person is totally deprived of the pleasantness and playfulness of daydreaming? To the contrary: a self-disciplined person knows when and where to daydream, and when and where to stay focused. Lisa Lathrop is a successful credit manager who daydreams while walking to and from appointments in her office. She also takes an occasional daydreaming break when shifting from one task to another.

Better Management of Personal Finances

Many people blame their financial problems on low income, high expenses, or a combination of the two. Yet many people with comparable income and expenses are able to avoid financial troubles. The difference is that self-disciplined people are able to stick to a spending plan (a.k.a. budget). Such people carefully compare planned expenses to anticipated income, and then pare down expenses to match income. Of more fundamental importance, financially self-uisciplined people do not spend more than they earn. For example, the self-disciplined person might squeeze one more year out of an old car until she has enough money to purchase a new car.

PEOPLE WHO CONTROL THEIR EXPENSES THROUGH BUDGETING HAVE MORE FUN WITH THEIR MONEY.

Another staple of the financially self-disciplined is to set aside money for savings and investments, or a reserve before paying other bills. An objection many people raise to closely following a spending plan is that restricting yourself financially hampers fun and spontaneity. In reality, people who control their expenses through budgeting have more fun with their money. A vacation, "surround-sound" home entertainment center, or restaurant meal is more enjoyable when paid for immediately rather than by lingering credit-card payments. Financially self-disciplined people can afford to pay cash (or pay off the credit-card balance in 30 days) because they are often debt-free. The money otherwise used for interest payments is used for investments and luxuries. Imagine the fun of paying cash for a camcorder, car, or European vacation.

Better Relationships with Loved Ones

Just as self-disciplined people make more reliable work associates, they make better family members and close friends. The reliability factor is particularly important. Self-disciplined parents might say to a teenage child, "If you get into the college of your choice, we'll make sure the money is there when you need it." They will stay focused on the goal of providing adequate financial support, while their child focuses his energy on gaining acceptance to the school of his choice.

Another notable aspect of the reliability of self-disciplined people is their thoughtfulness. If a self-disciplined person's goal is to make a significant other happy, he will demonstrate that commitment in many ways. Demonstrations of commitment might include:

- Remembering birthdays and anniversaries
- Suggesting a return to a restaurant where the two people shared an especially romantic evening
- Wearing the outfit the partner likes so much
- Making arrangements to stay at the same hotel and same room where the couple had a fabulous getaway weekend earlier in the relationship
- Arranging work so the two can get together for dinner at an agreed upon time

Avoiding Altercations with the Law

Criminal behavior cannot be attributed exclusively to a lack of self-discipline, yet self-disciplined people tend to avoid actions that create legal problems. A case in point is frequent traffic violators. Because of their inability to control their speeding or driving while intoxicated, the inveterate traffic law violator has to take time off from work to appear in court. As the tickets amass, the person is forced to spend outrageous sums for auto insurance. Instead of having money to invest in true fun, the violator must spend a large chunk of income on insurance.

12

Overcoming Socioeconomic Disadvantages
and Discrimination

A number of conservative ideologists believe that many problems of socioeconomic disadvantages and discrimination are better cured by self-discipline than government intervention. According to the politically conservative analysis, self-reliance and self-discipline are the major factors that will enable people to overcome cultural and socioeconomic disadvantages.

Racism is presumably not a factor in this argument. Caucasian and African-American conservatives alike offer the same prescriptions. Part of the argument is that many people do conquer poverty, cultural disadvantages, and racism to create a good life for themselves. With the right amount of self-discipline others from the same background could do likewise.

Washington Post columnist William Raspberry is concerned that too many African-Americans blame racism for their problems, using excuses such as: "If it weren't for racism I would have had my promotion by now. I wouldn't have been stopped for speeding, and if I had I certainly wouldn't have been given that big a ticket. You think that cop would have arrested me for what I said if I'd been white?" In response to these comments, Raspberry says:

> I hear the recitals—the excuses—and I find them as fanciful as my dreams for winning the lottery and getting in shape. Most of the things complained of would be considerably eased by some combination of exertion, self-discipline, and mouth control. Racism serves as sort of generalized rationalization for not trying.[8]

Whether you accept Raspberry's reasoning or not, it does underscore the role of self-discipline in overcoming barriers to success. The self-disciplined person might say, "I know that racism (or ageism, or antifemale prejudice, or discrimination against gays or lesbians) exists, and that it is hurting me. Yet with a commitment to excellence, I can improve my position in life just like thousands of others in my situation."

Assessing Your Current Level of Self-Discipline

Before proceeding with a general framework for developing self-discipline, you are invited to take the Self-Discipline Audit on page 15. It will provide you with initial insights into your present tendencies toward behaving and thinking like people with high self-discipline. Then, take the quiz again in six months to see how your attitudes and behavior have changed. I recommend a period of six months because it generally takes at least that long for complex change to be incorporated into everyday behavior.

THE EIGHT COMPONENTS OF SELF-DISCIPLINE

Since self-discipline is an ability, it can be learned and improved upon. My research has identified eight primary components, which comprise the model I'm going to take you through, step by step. Using the model requires hard work, concentration, and perhaps a substantial shift in philosophy and attitude. Another challenge will be to keep the eight components working together by attending to them all—all of the time. But I know you'll find it's worth the effort.

Component 1: Formulate a Mission Statement. Who are you? What are you trying to accomplish in life? What is your purpose in life? If you understand what you are trying to accomplish in life you have the fuel to be self-disciplined. Without a mission, it is too easy to drift away from goal attainment. *With* a mission, activities that may appear mundane to others become vital stepping-stones for you.

(*text continues on page 18*)

THE SELF-DISCIPLINE AUDIT

On the following scale, indicate the extent to which each of the following statements describes your behavior or attitude by circling one number for each: disagree strongly (DS); disagree (D); neutral (N); agree (A); agree strongly (AS). Consider asking someone who knows your behavior and attitudes well to help you respond accurately.

	DS	D	N	A	AS
1. I have a strong sense of purpose.	1	2	3	4	5
2. Life's a drag when you are always chasing goals.	5	4	3	2	1
3. My long-range plans in life are well established.	1	2	3	4	5
4. I feel energized when I have a new goal to pursue.	1	2	3	4	5
5. It is difficult for me to picture an event in my mind before it occurs.	5	4	3	2	1
6. When success is near, I can almost taste, feel, and see it.	1	2	3	4	5
7. I consult my daily planner or a to-do list almost every work day.	1	2	3	4	5
8. My days rarely turn out the way I had planned.	5	4	3	2	1
9. What I do for a living isn't nearly as important as the money it pays.	5	4	3	2	1
10. Some parts of my job are as exciting to me as any hobby or pastime.	1	2	3	4	5

audit continues

	DS	D	N	A	AS
11. Working 60 hours per week for even a short period of time would be out of the question for me.	5	4	3	2	1
12. I have personally known several people who would be good role models for me.	1	2	3	4	5
13. So far I have never read about or known anybody whose lifestyle I'd like to emulate.	5	4	3	2	1
14. My work is so demanding that it's difficult for me to concentrate fully on my personal life when I'm at home.	5	4	3	2	1
15. When I'm involved in an important work project, I can enjoy myself fully at a sporting or cultural event after hours.	1	2	3	4	5
16. If it weren't for a few bad breaks, I would be much more successful today.	5	4	3	2	1
17. My best helping hand is at the end of my arm.	1	2	3	4	5
18. I get bored easily.	5	4	3	2	1
19. Planning is difficult because life is so unpredictable.	5	4	3	2	1
20. I feel that I'm moving forward a little bit every day toward achieving my goals.	1	2	3	4	5

audit continues

Scoring and Interpretation

Calculate your score by adding up the numbers circled. If you scored:

90–100 points

You are a highly self-disciplined person who should be able to capitalize on your skills and talents. Continue reading for your enjoyment. Like most self-disciplined people, you will probably achieve additional insight into things you already do well or know.

60–89 points

You have an average degree of self-discipline. Keep reading! You're sure to acquire new ideas for improving your self-discipline.

40–59 points

You may be experiencing problems with self-discipline. Start putting into practice the suggestions you read here as soon as you can.

1–39 points

If your answers are accurate, you have enough problems with self-discipline to limit achieving many of the things in life important to you. Along with this book, I suggest reading one on work habits and time management.

The Self-Discipline Model

Since a mission statement is equivalent to a general purpose in life, a personal strategy (master plan), or a lifetime goal statement, formulating one can be intellectually and spiritually uplifting. Committing your mission statement to paper or computer screen facilitates its clarification and refinement. Virtually all successful people have either a written statement of their mission or a mental version they can access immediately. Bill Gates, the chairman of Microsoft Corp., has stated frequently that he wants to help the world make better use of information. Building a world-class software company has been his way to fulfill that mission.

Cora, a temporary office worker, noticed that Kitty, one of the professionals in the office where she was assigned, was constantly seated in front of a computer. One day when Kitty returned from lunch, Cora engaged her in general conversation about the weather and commuting. Kitty looked down at her watch, and said, "Excuse me. I have to get back to work."

Cora commented, "Excuse me for saying so, but don't you get bored just sitting in front of a computer all day?" Kitty smiled and replied, "It may look like I'm just sitting in front of a computer banging the keyboard. But my computer is a tool that helps me accomplish something very important. I'm analyzing data to help determine how our company can make our products more environmentally friendly. In this way, I'm helping to improve the world."

At the mention of a mission statement, many people visualize spending a long weekend in the woods, engulfing themselves in nature, and hoping for inspiration. In reality, about 60 minutes of solitude is sufficient for getting your personal mission on paper. To get you started, I'd like you to write down the two questions that follow, and answer them spontaneously. Spontaneous comments, even frivolous ones, are often the most revealing and truthful. Try to avoid preconceived limitations—they may prevent you from making the bold moves that could be necessary to fulfill a mission.

A labor union official in Detroit for many years dreamed of becoming an attorney. But he was always held back by what he saw as his limitation: Without a college degree he would never be admitted to an accredited law school. Finally, though, in a fit of determination, he declared to himself and his family that his strongest career desire was to become an attorney. And, after making many telephone calls and faxing messages, he learned that a nearby law school accepted law-related experience as a substitute for a college degree. He applied to the law school, was accepted, graduated, and is now a successful attorney in private practice.

1. *What are my five biggest wishes in life?*

Be as honest and bold as you can in identifying these five wishes. You are not committing yourself to achieving all of them, but fantasy wishes point toward an ideal life. Here are some wishes people have shared with me:

- Retire from work at age 45, as a multimillionaire.
- Fly around the world in my private jet, overseeing my many investments.
- Have a vacation mansion in southern France, a ski condo in Colorado, and a penthouse apartment in San Francisco, overlooking the Bay.
- Win one golf tournament a year.

2. *What do I want to accomplish in my career during the next five years?*

Write down whatever comes into your head—impose no limits. Describe what you want to accomplish for yourself or for your employer: a promotion, increase in salary, an improved gross profit margin for your company, etc.

Your answers to these two broad questions are the raw data for formulating a crisp mission statement of about twenty-five words. Company mission statements, as well as mission statements for work teams, follow a similar format. It helps define your place in the world, and represents your intense desires. A mission propels you toward self-discipline because every completed task is one more step toward achieving your mission.

Component 2: Develop Role Models. An excellent method of learning how to be self-disciplined is to model your behavior after successful achievers who are obviously well-disciplined. To model another person does not mean you will slavishly imitate every detail of that person's life. Instead, you will follow the general pattern of how the person operates in spheres related to your mission and goals.

20

SAMPLE MISSION STATEMENTS

Business Communication Specialist: To become a well-recognized professional in my field, known for her extraordinary ability to advise management on issues relating to ethics and social responsibility. Expect to become regional v.p. of my professional association. Want to be admired by my family.

Information Systems Analyst: To be known as a key figure in my company, leading the path toward reengineering the corporation, and helping link our company electronically with a variety of beneficial partners. Want to be recognized as a model family person who also gives something important back to his community.

An assistant buyer intent on strengthening his self-discipline has adopted Pat Riley (the coach of the Knicks) as a role model:

Coach Riley is the coolest. He knows exactly what he wants to accomplish each time his team takes the floor. Riley is impeccably dressed and his hair is always neat. The man never loses emotional control. At the beginning of a basketball season, Riley holds his first practice session as early as the league rules allow. That means 12:01 a.m. on the first possible day. Riley said during one season, "I want my team to be the first on the court this season, and the last off." He meant that his team would win the championship. They did reach the final game of the NBA championship against the Houston Rockets (1993–94 season).

An important point about selecting a role model or a mentor is choosing a person whose level of success will stretch your capability. Your role model should reflect the level of achievement that will lead you toward completing your mission. An ideal role model is the type of person whom you would like to become, not someone you feel you could never become. You should choose new role models every few years because the approach to developing self-discipline is dynamic: It will change as your life circumstances change. Developing self-discipline is a lifelong process of continuous improvement.

Suitable role models can be found in your company, industry, high school, college, or community. You can also find a role model in books, magazines, newspapers, on radio or television. A major criterion is that you absorb enough information about that person so you can pattern yourself after his or her tightly focused persistence toward reaching goals.

Donna Karan, of Donna Karan Inc., exemplifies a business executive who is a role model for many women in the fashion industry. Karan is one of the few well-known women in the male-dominated world of U.S. clothing design. Her business units include top-of-the-line fashions for both men and women, sportswear, and children's clothing.

Karan attracts talented people to her firm, who become fiercely loyal to her and are willing to put up with her demands for perfection. Two of her key executives have been with Karan since her days at Anne Klein. Her executive assistant says, "Donna draws you in. She's this irresistible force." Most of her staff have become somewhat of a Donna Karan cult. A vice president for design says, "Everyone loves what she does and wants to dress like her and be like her."[10]

Riley and Karan have been presented as high-profile role models. You can also develop role models of self-disciplined, high achievers who are playing in lesser leagues. A department head, parent, or relative can be the perfect role model of self-discipline.

Component 3: Develop Goals for Each Task. The third component of developing self-discipline stems logically from the first. Your mission must be supported by a series of specific goals that

22

collectively will enable you to achieve your mission. All non-Martians reading this book have already studied or heard about goal-setting or have incorporated goal-setting into their job! Perhaps less familiar to you, however, is the best-documented fact about human behavior: Setting difficult and specific goals improves performance. Goal-setting is therefore as important to the self-disciplined achiever as an engine is to a vehicle.

Another interesting scientific fact about goals is that they have an arousal effect on the brain. When you establish challenging goals, your heart rate increases, and as the heart rate increases, you become more mentally aroused or energized to reach the goal. The arousal appears to be related to setting higher goals and producing more.[11] Setting goals thus becomes a self-feeding success cycle.

If carried to completion, the self-feeding success cycle would work this way: You set a challenging goal → You experience physiological arousal in attempting to reach your goal → You produce more and set higher goals → You experience more arousal → You set still higher goals and produce even more → You eventually reach your mission → You modify or create another mission or uplift the original one.

Successfully completing goals eventually leads to fulfilling a mission. In the interim, it is necessary to set goals for each task to stay focused on what you are trying to accomplish. Each small goal achieved is a building block toward larger achievements. Self-disciplined people are characteristically good with details because they realize every small task has to be done right for overall success. Donna Karan, for example, stalks the model runway when she presents a seasonal collection to fashion buyers. She is in constant motion behind the curtain, tucking, smoothing, and adjusting angles unnoticeable to others. Her clear intent is to stay on top of every detail, even if she is the company president.

Much of the wisdom of setting workable goals can be boiled down to a straightforward principle: *Specify what is going to be accomplished, who is going to accomplish it, when it is going to be accomplished, and how it is going to be accomplished.* Establishing the what, who, when, and how of your goals gives you a clear mental image of what you are trying to accomplish, thus helping you focus your efforts. Here is a goal statement from a sales manager at a camera company: "I will be responsible for increasing sales of digital cameras by 50 percent within 12 months. Returns will be subtracted from the dollar amounts of sales. Only those sales will count for the total that have actually been delivered to the customer."

Component 4: Develop Action Plans to Achieve Goals. The "how" in goal-setting leads logically to developing step-by-step plans to achieve the goals. Self-disciplined people carefully follow their action plans because they make goal attainment possible. For instance, part of the sales manager's action plan for increasing the sale of digital cameras might be an advertising program or conducting market research about potential customers.

It is helpful to chart your progress against the dates established for the subactivities. The sales manager's time and activity chart (see illustration on page 25) indicates that he is on target with several activities, such as meeting with the advertising executive and conducting the focus group. Launching the ad campaign and beginning telemarketing, however, are running behind schedule. If the sales manager has strong self-discipline, he will frequently consult the time and activity chart to detect events that are falling behind schedule and move quickly to rectify the situation.

Gary Webb, the manager of Nik and the Nice Guys, a rock band with local and national gigs, is highly self-disciplined. He uses high technology to take care of small tasks so he can concentrate on larger tasks with high potential payout to the

TIME AND ACTIVITY CHART FOR SELLING DIGITAL CAMERAS

Activity	Jan 15	Feb 15	Mar 15	Apr 15	May 15
Meet with advertising executive	P A				
Launch ad campaign		P	A		
Conduct focus group		P A			
Prepare report on focus group		P	A		
Hire one telemarketer			P A		
Begin telemarketing				P	A

P = planned date
A = actual date of accomplishment

band. By using voice mail, fax machines, and high-output copiers he is able to worry less about clerical chores and concentrate on bookings. Part of his self-discipline involves developing action plans to increase bookings. Gary formulated a detailed networking system to increase bookings, where he regularly charts progress against goals. When he bought a new computer system for the band he established contacts at the computer corporation. Capitalizing on these contacts, Gary struck a gig for Nik and the Nice Guys at one of the computer company's annual conventions.

As part of the networking system, all performers and road crew are given business cards with one stipulation: "Don't give out a card without getting one in return." If the contact results in a booked gig, the individual is rewarded with a percentage of the booking. All gigs and potential bookings are maintained in a database and distributed to band road crew members regularly. (If you didn't expect rock musicians to be well-disciplined business-people, you could still be right. Most members of Nik and the Nice Guys have day jobs like accountant, lawyer, and computer specialist.)

Component 5: Use Visual and Sensory Simulation. A self-disciplined person relentlessly focuses on a goal and persistently pursues that goal. To accomplish this consistent focus, self-disciplined people form images of reaching their goal—they actually develop a mental image of the act of accomplishing what they want. As mysterious as it sounds, visualization helps the brain convert images into reality.

Have you ever noticed, for example, that if you concentrate hard enough you can reproduce an aroma? The reproduction of an aroma is possible even though there is no real physical stimulation from the smell receptors in the nose, through a nerve pathway up to the brain. If you visualize your favorite perfume or cologne, your nose is not stimulated by particulates of those substances. Your visualization leads to a simulation which triggers the brain into reproducing the sensation of smell. As smart as the brain might be, it is tricked into confusing a mental image with a physical reality.

AS MYSTERIOUS AS IT SOUNDS, VISUALIZATION HELPS THE BRAIN CONVERT IMAGES INTO REALITY.

How does visualization really work? Take the example of a self-disciplined person who wants to complete painting a sundeck by sundown. He would visualize standing next to a freshly painted deck as the sun slips down beneath the horizon, imagining how relaxing it feels having the deck painted and being able to put away the painting supplies.

The more senses you can incorporate into your visual image, the stronger its power. Imagine yourself seeing, tasting, hearing, smelling, and touching your goal. The sales manager attempting to increase the sales of digital cameras might visualize hundreds of digital cameras being shipped from the warehouse and imagine what the food served at the victory banquet would taste like. He would visualize hearing the vice president of marketing say, "Great job. We're proud of you," and imagine what it would be like to accept a bonus check and shake hands with the V.P.

Frequent rehearsal is an important aspect of visual and sensory simulations. For instance, successful athletes constantly rehearse making a key shot in the closing seconds of a game or match. The football kicker rehearses kicking a field goal as the clock runs out hundreds of times. Visualization does not bring 100 percent success, but it does increase the odds of achieving your goal.

Moments of victory in business and personal life can also be rehearsed. The new sales professional might rehearse a scenario with a prospective customer: "If you write a check today, I am authorized to give you a 5 percent cash discount. That will save your company $375."

The frustrated parent might visualize a winning tactic when her child throws a tantrum in the supermarket. Instead of clobbering the child and creating a bigger stir, the parent rehearses saying: "I love you, but I hate the way you're acting now. We're not moving from this spot until you quiet down."

Rehearsal also helps lower anxiety surrounding a challenging situation. Anxiety decreases because familiarity—achieved through rehearsing—makes it less threatening. Many people, for example, are anxious the first time they run a new piece of software. After awhile, learning new software loses its anxiety-provoking properties because it has become a familiar experience.

Lowering anxiety builds confidence and control, which, in turn, makes it easier to ask for the sale or make the winning shot. Using rehearsal to lower anxiety is so valuable that it has become a standard technique for helping people become more assertive in demanding situations.

Component 6: Search for Pleasure Within the Task. A self-disciplined person finds joy, excitement, and intense involvement in the task at hand. The love of the task helps the person persist in pursuit of the goal. An axiom of becoming wealthy is not to focus on getting rich. Instead, focus on a type of work you enjoy passionately. Riches are a by-product of doing exciting and enjoyable work.

Even if you aren't fortunate enough to be doing work you find intensely enjoyable, you aren't excluded from task enjoyment. The saving tactic is to search for the most enjoyable elements within a job or task, although much of the job or task is drudging. Consider the paralegal striving to develop more self-discipline. Although she dislikes preparing figures for a house closing, she enjoys collecting necessary information from lawyers, clients, bank personnel, and county employees. Reflecting on how much she enjoys this aspect of the task furnishes enough of a high to sustain her motivation for completing the task on time.

Component 7: Compartmentalize Spheres of Life. Self-disciplined people have a remarkable capacity to divide up (or compartmentalize) the various spheres of their lives to stay focused on what they are doing at the moment. Without concentrating on one sphere of life at a time, the various roles a person occupies interfere with each other. Interference is more pronounced when problems occur in a major sphere of life. For example, a manufacturing engineer facing a crisis at the plant might find it difficult to effectively listen to her child's concerns about a kindergarten teacher. Yet if she could learn to block out thoughts about the work emergency while at home, she could listen intently to her child.

A self-disciplined person develops the knack of concentrating on one task at a time. While on the job, she strives to think only about work—at least in the midst of a task. Between tasks, she might think about off-the-job activities. When in the middle of a personal activity requiring full attention, she devotes full attention to that activity. Off-the-job activities that don't require full attention, such as washing a car, allow ample opportunity for thinking about work.

A negative consequence of not being able to compartmentalize is that task performance and enjoyment both suffer. Ruminating about a broken romance while preparing a report can result in a slipshod report. And ruminating over a political squabble in the office while on vacation can result in your being a poor vacation companion.

Learning to compartmentalize requires mind control. Faced with interviewing a job candidate, tell yourself: "OK, this interview requires my 100 percent attention. I'll give it my best shot." Should your attention drift as the candidate begins to talk about his or her job experiences, say to yourself, "Stop, you're losing focus."

A related technique for compartmentalizing is to use visual focusing. Assume you're seated at a computer, entering important information into a file. Earlier in the morning you received a disturbing phone call from your auto dealer, who said your car needs $780 worth of repairs to pass inspection. You are already over budget for the month. Indeed, you are facing a problem, but now is the time to enter data into the computer. Stare intently at the most recent row of data you entered. Keep staring until it's the only thought on your mind. After your attention is pinpointed on the data, move on with the task of entering more data.

Component 8: Minimize Excuse Making. Self-disciplined people concentrate their energies on goal accomplishment, rather than making excuses for why work is not accomplished. Instead of trying to justify why they've been diverted from a goal, the high-achieving, self-disciplined person circumvents potential barriers. Undisciplined people, in contrast, seem to look for excuses. Here, for example, is a sampling of the excuses cigarette smokers make for not following through with their plans to quit smoking:

"I was doing fine until Thanksgiving and Christmas came along. *Nobody* gives up smoking during the holiday season."

29

"I read that people who give up smoking wind up gaining loads of weight. That's worse than smoking."

"I was all set to quit for good when I developed marital problems. How can you quit smoking in the middle of a crisis?"

"The Tobacco Institute recently questioned the scientific accuracy of some of the antismoking studies. I'd like to see more conclusive evidence about the bad effects of smoking before I quit."

Are you an excuse maker? Why not conduct a self-audit, writing down all the reasons blocking you from achieving any current goal. Be brutally honest in challenging each one of your excuses. Ask yourself, "Is this a valid excuse, or is it simply a rationalization for my getting sidetracked?"

Up to this point I have described the benefits of self-discipline and given you a chance to measure your tendencies toward self-discipline. Most importantly, you have been presented with the major components of the self-discipline model. Incorporate these into your work and personal life and you will have learned the key to success. However, your journey toward becoming a self-disciplined high achiever is not complete. We move next to deeper understandings of how to capture the transforming power of self-discipline.

LIVING BY THE REALITY PRINCIPLE

Self-disciplined people are able *and* willing to put aside immediate pleasure to achieve a long-range goal. Rather than divert their efforts by a quick fix, they patiently work toward the bigger payoff that comes later. For instance, in the midst of a job search, the less-disciplined person will accept the first offer that comes along, even if it pays less than what she needs and does not contribute to career growth.

If you can postpone immediate pleasure and short-term relief from pain to achieve a long-term benefit, you are operating by the reality principle. If you are concerned primarily with short-term pleasure and immediate avoidance of discomfort, you are operating by the pleasure principle. To become a self-disciplined person, you must learn to operate primarily by the reality principle.

An in-depth understanding of the difference between the reality and pleasure principles will help you in your quest to strengthen your self-discipline. And the best source for that is Sigmund Freud.

FREUD'S EXPLANATION

Actually, it was the classic philosophers who first described the reality and pleasure principles. (Being a highly self-disciplined person, Sigmund Freud used the Greek philosophers, Socrates, Plato, and Aristotle, as effective role models for many of his ideas.) It all begins with an understanding of the role of the id in personality.[1] According to Freud, the id is the "seething cauldron" of unconscious urges and desires that continually seek expression. The id is the source of all psychic energy and the primitive system out of which evolve the other parts of personality.

IF YOU CAN POSTPONE IMMEDIATE PLEASURE AND SHORT-TERM RELIEF FROM PAIN TO ACHIEVE A LONG-TERM BENEFIT, YOU ARE OPERATING BY THE REALITY PRINCIPLE.

Two main classes of instincts stem from the id: life instincts and death instincts. Life instincts are concerned with survival—hunger, thirst, and especially sex. Death instincts are concerned with destructive impulses, which take the form of aggression. The id impulses are blind, brutish, irrational demands for immediate gratification. The id adheres to the pleasure principle by trying to obtain immediate gratification, thus pursuing pleasure and avoiding pain.

Because the id has no contact with the real world, it is limited to finding immediate gratification in two ways. One gratifier is the reflex action, such as coughing or sneezing, which relieves unpleasant sensations at once. The other gratifier is wishful thinking, or primary-process thinking, where you form a mental image of a person, object, or situation that partially satisfies the instinct or the discomfort. Primary-process thinking is primitive and does not use logic or intelligence.

Since the id is incapable of satisfying the biological instincts it contains, the personality develops the ego. The ego serves to mediate between instinctual impulses and reality. It redirects and controls impulses so that actual gratification can be achieved. The ego works for the id by showing it how to satisfy raw impulses in socially acceptable ways. The ego operates on conscious and unconscious levels and is capable of perceiving, thinking, planning, and deciding.

The ego controls thinking and reasoning activities. It is also the part of the human personality that learns about the external world through the senses. The ego faces the challenge of controlling the id's drives in the external world and takes on the role of intermediary. A person's basic instincts are demanding gratification, and the ego takes on the role of telling the person when and how to satisfy these impulses. (See figure on page 34.)

In contrast to the pleasure principle, the ego adheres to, or obeys, the reality principle. By using logical reasoning, the ego attempts to delay satisfying the id's desire until it can do so safely and successfully. Freud called this secondary-process thinking.

When the individual attempts to satisfy its basic impulses, he or she runs into conflict with the rules and values of society. These rules and values are made clear to the child by how the parent and other influential people react to the child's behavior. As a result, the superego gradually develops in the child. The superego is a system of controlling and inhibiting forces against the basic impulses of aggression and sex that could be disruptive to society. The superego eventually becomes the conscious that substitutes for the external forces of parental and societal control. Here we are less concerned about the superego than the id and ego, because the id and ego are directly linked to the pleasure and reality principles.

The Pleasure Principle Versus the Reality Principle

How the Pleasure Principle Operates

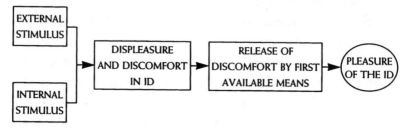

How the Reality Principle Operates

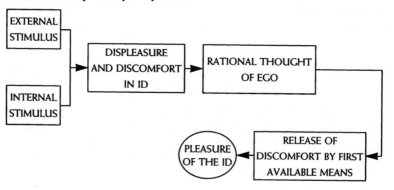

The Freudian theory of personality has parallels to understanding self-discipline. Self-disciplined people adhere closely to the reality principle because they want long-term, constructive solutions to their problems. (People lacking in self-discipline, of course, do not operate *entirely* by the pleasure principle. If they did they would be wild, primitive, uninhibited, and unfit for society.)

A person with high self-discipline who works in a company that is downsizing would do everything in her power to acquire the skills needed to find new employment, even though it means taking more time in the job-search process. A person with low self-discipline instead of taking action might fantasize about achieving a promotion—despite the fact that jobs are being lost.

(Although a promotion is not a biological urge, it is a modern way of achieving a variety of pleasures.)

Following the reality principle does not exclude satisfaction of your primitive urges. Instead, you satisfy these urges in a way that serves your best long-term interests. For example, a manufacturer who operates by the pleasure principle might achieve short-range gain by selling his product with low-quality components. By operating by the reality principle, he would use higher-quality components, thus taking a small profit. Yet by building a quality reputation he will stay in business longer and earn greater profits over a long time period.

To examine your tendency to operate by the reality principle, take the self-quiz on page 36. When you complete it you'll find a discussion of each of the ten statements.

USING THE REALITY PRINCIPLE IN PLANNING YOUR CAREER

Career planning is one sphere of life which lends itself readily to the reality principle. The most basic application of the reality principle in career planning is the contribution of formal education to a person's long-range career. A high-school graduate will enjoy the immediate gratification of money by obtaining a job at close to minimum wage. By obtaining a two-year degree at a career school or junior college, her lifetime earnings will double. Job satisfaction will also increase. By earning a four-year college degree, she has the opportunity of advancing into higher-level positions. Since executive positions pay about two to three times as much as technical positions, a career-planner with the self-discipline to complete college (or graduate education) might triple or quadruple her lifetime earnings.

The story of chiropractor Richard Sidor illustrates how the reality principle is an asset in career planning. Sidor, age 33, is

(text continues on page 44)

THE REALITY PRINCIPLE SELF-QUIZ

Circle the alternative to each question that most accurately reflects how you would probably act, or what you would advise, in the situation described. Your spontaneous answer is likely to be the most accurate.

1. Guests are scheduled to arrive at your home for dinner in about two hours. You have run short of the gourmet sauce you are using to prepare dinner. Your solution is to:
   a. substitute a bottle of ketchup for the sauce, mixing it well with what remains.
   b. run to the store for a new bottle of sauce, and explain to your guests that dinner will be 20 minutes late.
   c. make less sauce, and then serve smaller portions to the guests.
   d. quickly telephone one of the guests and ask him to run to the store, and bring the sauce over as soon as possible.

2. You are taking an evening course while working full time. A course requirement is to write a paper, due in three weeks. Suddenly you become swamped at work, and you don't know how you can get the paper done on time. Your solution is to:
   a. get up one hour earlier each day for the next 30 days, to give you the necessary time to write the paper.
   b. explain the circumstances to your instructor and ask for an incomplete grade.
   c. drop the course in order to perform well on your job.
   d. explain the situation to your boss, and ask to postpone one of your assignments for 30 days.

quiz continues

3. Jeremy is an industrial sales representative whose goal is to become a marketing vice president. His company offers him an assistant manager position in company headquarters. Two days after accepting the offer, he receives an offer from a competitive company to join them as a sales representative. The commission structure would allow him to earn about one-third more than he has been earning at his current job. Jeremy should:

   a. take the offer to his present company, saying he will stay providing he receives a 33⅓ percent salary increase.

   b. grab the offer with the other company immediately.

   c. take the offer to his present company, and ask if he can return to his sales representative position with a commission plan that would increase his earnings by about one-third.

   d. politely decline the offer from the competitor explaining that he wants to pursue a career in management with his present company.

4. You are at a party with a casual date, in whom you have very little interest. While chatting with a group of people, a highly attractive stranger approaches you and says, "Drop your escort and come along with me." You say to the stranger:

   a. "That's out of the question, but I'd like to hear from you."

   b. "Your place or mine?"

   c. "Get lost."

   d. "I can't but let's at least go outside for a quick drink."

quiz continues

37 ·

5. You plan to work most of the weekend on an important report due Monday morning. Your spouse announces that a friend has just given the two of you tickets to a Saturday night show you have been dying to see. You say to your spouse:

   a. "I'm sorry I can't make it: business before pleasure. Why don't you ask your sister to go with you?"

   b. "Great idea. It will make me two days late with my report, but I'm sure the company won't go under because of it."

   c. "What a great opportunity. I can do it as long as I devote the rest of the weekend to preparing my report."

   d. "I'll join you for the second act."

6. You have been invited to join your company's strategic planning task force. You are thrilled, except that joining the committee means you'll have to participate in a weekend retreat—an activity you think you would despise. Your decision is to:

   a. decline the invitation rather than sacrifice a weekend.

   b. accept the assignment, and just bite the bullet for the weekend retreat.

   c. accept the invitation with the qualifier that you will not be available to participate in the retreat.

   d. accept the invitation with the qualifier that you can attend the retreat for Saturday only.

7. As a middle manager, you make frequent presentations to top management and rely heavily on visual displays provided by the art department. Top management lays off that department. From now on all middle managers and professionals have to prepare their own computer graphics and slides. You'll have to learn how to use computer

quiz continues

38

graphics, an area in which you have zero knowledge. Your decision is to:

   a. go back to making simple flip-chart presentations.

   b. take a 15-week course in computer graphics on your own time.

   c. hire a student computer whiz to help you whenever you need to make a presentation.

   d. skip the visuals in your future presentations.

8. Gradually your debts have become so high that your monthly income doesn't cover them. Your solution is to:

   a. get a consolidation loan so your monthly payments will be smaller, although you'll be paying on the consolidation loan for six years.

   b. keep mushrooming your debt until your income catches up with your monthly bills.

   c. deprive yourself of new clothing and almost all entertainment until you can pay off at least one debt.

   d. each month skip paying one bill without letting any bill go unpaid for two consecutive months.

9. Owing to a political squabble, you have lost your job. Between your severance pay and the cushion you have accumulated, you estimate you can last nine months without a salary. Your decision is to:

   a. take two months to contemplate your future, and then begin a job hunt.

   b. play it cool and hope that somebody will come after you with a job offer.

   c. begin immediately looking for a job, and take any part-time, temporary work you can find for about 20 hours per week.

   d. write letters to all the people in your network, asking them to offer you a job.

quiz continues

10. You and your significant other have been invited to a posh dinner Saturday night at 9:00 p.m. You find it uncomfortable to wait until past 7:00 p.m. to eat, yet you strongly want to attend this dinner. You decide to:
    a. attend the dinner, but have a light meal at 6:00 p.m. to tide you over.
    b. ask the hosts if they could serve dinner at 7:30 p.m.
    c. drink alcoholic beverages early Saturday night until you lose your appetite.
    d. eat two pieces of fruit early Saturday night, and then attend the dinner.

Scoring and Interpretation

The points for each answer are as follows:

1.	a.	0	5.	a.	5
	b.	10		b.	0
	c.	5		c.	10
	d.	2		d.	2
2.	a.	10	6.	a.	9
	b.	3		b.	10
	c.	2		c.	0
	d.	1		d.	1
3.	a.	1	7.	a.	1
	b.	1		b.	10
	c.	1		c.	6
	d.	10		d.	0
4.	a.	10	8.	a.	7
	b.	0		b.	0
	c.	0		c.	10
	d.	4		d.	1

quiz continues

40

9. a.	0	10. a.	5
b.	2	b.	0
c.	10	c.	0
d.	4	d.	10

85–100 points: You have a remarkably strong reality principle.

54–84 points: You have a moderate reality principle.

0–53 points: You have a strong pleasure principle.

Question 1: Alternative "b" reflects a strong reality principle. The host chooses an alternative that will delay the dinner shortly but will work much better than a quick fix such as pouring ketchup into the sauce.

Question 2: Alternative "a" reflects a strong reality principle. You are incurring the inconvenience of getting up one hour earlier each day for 30 days to accomplish a task that could have a significant impact on your future—successfully completing a course.

Question 3: Alternative "d" reflects an important application of the reality principle. Jeremy would obtain immediate pleasure from the higher income he would receive by joining the competitor. By so doing, however, he would forgo an opportunity to take an important step toward becoming a marketing executive. The assistant manager position puts Jeremy's career on the right path to attain his goals. Notice also that by choosing alternative "d" Jeremy is not burning his bridges—he is saying he might say yes next time.

Question 4: Alternative "a" is a good application of the reality principle. Your id is probably crying out to drop your date and take off with the attractive stranger, yet you have let common decency and the reality principle take control. However, this doesn't preclude your developing a relationship with the attractive stranger.

quiz continues

41

Question 5: Alternative "c" is a sensible application of the reality principle. Attending the show and pleasing your spouse are important to you, yet meeting your work obligations are also necessary. You have chosen to bypass the immediate pleasure of attending the show and worrying about the report later. A high degree of self-discipline will enable you to complete the report by effective use of every spare moment this weekend.

Question 6: Alternative "b" is clearly the best application of the reality principle. You would avoid short-range discomfort by not having to attend the retreat, yet you would frustrate your intermediate-range goal of wanting to become part of the elite task force. Biting the bullet for the retreat is worthwhile. While you are there, don't forget one of the key components of self-discipline: search for pleasure within the task.

Question 7: Alternative "b" reflects an action based on the reality principle. You are willing to endure the inconvenience of taking a 15-week course in computer graphics so that you can continue to make high-quality presentations to management. Hiring a student to do the work for you (alternative "c") also reflects a tactic based on the reality principle. Yet your long-term interests will be better served by developing the skills yourself.

Question 8: Alternative "c" reflects the clearest application of the reality principle. You have the self-discipline to endure the short-term inconvenience of depriving yourself of some purchases and entertainment so you can begin digging yourself out of debt. Your long-term mental health is best served by pursuing this alternative. The consolidation loan (alternative "a") also has merit but it increases the amount of time you will remain in debt.

Question 9: Alternative "c" is the clearest application of the reality principle. Instead of delaying or avoiding the tough task of conducting a job search, you are digging right in. Your quest for
quiz continues

part-time, temporary work also shows that you are concerned about the long-term effect of being unemployed: Your capital can erode quickly as you conduct a job search. Should you get into financial trouble, your peace of mind will be adversely affected.

Question 10: Alternative "d" reflects a simple, everyday application of the reality principle. Your needs for immediate gratification would be best served by eating a meal before attending the posh dinner. So doing, however, would deprive you of the long-term satisfaction of enjoying an elegant evening out with your partner.

married and has two preschool children. He has been in solo practice for six years, has just completed a two-year program in physical therapy, and is completing an internship.

Why would a licensed chiropractor also want a degree in physical therapy? According to Rick, of the two approaches to physical rehabilitation, physical therapy and chiropractic medicine, physical therapy is the most generally accepted by physicians and patients. When patients under the care of a physician reach the point where they need rehabilitation and physical restrengthening, many physicians do not make referrals to chiropractors. Insurance coverage is also better for physical therapy. Most medical insurance policies will not pay for rehabilitation and physical restrengthening by a chiropractor.

PEOPLE WHO ARE SUFFICIENTLY SELF-DISCIPLINED TO TAKE A LONG-RANGE PERSPECTIVE IN CAREER PLANNING WILL ACHIEVE LIFELONG BENEFITS.

Rick analyzed his predicament in these terms: "I said to myself that I could be frustrated like this for the next 30 to 40 years while practicing chiropractic medicine. My other alternative was to go through two years of hell and get the degree that would allow me to do the rehabilitation. After that training was completed, I could get the referrals I wanted and end the frustration."

Rick was accepted into a two-year program at a university that required a three-hour, round-trip commute. He attended classes two or three times a week and invested an average of 30 hours per week in study and related activities. He also invested about 40 to 50 hours per week in his chiropractic practice. Many weeks he devoted 85 hours a week to a combination of work and schooling. He routinely went to sleep at midnight and awoke at 4:30 a.m. to prepare for school and take care of office paperwork.

Rick knows he made many business and family sacrifices to reach his goal. He sacrificed time with his family, many hours of potential patient care, and time with his wife and children. Rick commented, "If you don't have the self-discipline, it just doesn't happen. You suffer a little bit in the short run to make up for it in the long run." He noted that there were many 20-year-old college students in the same program who failed although they had no other responsibilities.

Rick said he first acquired habits of self-discipline while playing high-school football. He said, "I got out of school at three o'clock and had football practice until six or seven. You couldn't goof off, watch TV, and go to bed. There was homework to do, otherwise you would fail the next day's quiz. Your grades would drop, and you would no longer be eligible to play."

Dr. Rick Sidor operates by the reality principle. To fit the external world's requirements of getting certification in physical therapy he made enormous short-term and intermediate-term sacrifices. His long-range future as an independent practitioner of chiropractic medicine and physical therapy now seems secure.

STAYING OUT OF TROUBLE

A powerful benefit of the self-discipline imposed by operating by the reality principle is that it helps you stay out of a variety of trouble. Keep your id under control and you might avoid a host of legal, financial, medical, interpersonal, and educational problems. A principal in an investment firm furnished this example:

The specialty of our firm is initial public offerings (IPOs). This means we are the underwriters for stocks of firms going public for the first time. IPOs are under scrutiny these days because a few firms in the industry have used some deceptive practices to lure clients. We therefore tell our investment consultants (sales representatives) to approach prospects with a high degree of professionalism. We want to guard against being perceived as a boiler-room operation.

Despite our warnings, occasionally one of our investment consultants will make outlandish claims for the expected returns from an IPO, intimating that the prospective client can expect yields of about 25 to 30 percent the first year. When a client does get duped, we hear about it in a big way. If we get more than a few complaints about an investment consultant, we terminate him or her. The consultant winds up getting fired from a potentially lucrative career with us. Just to make a quick commission, the guy or gal loses out on a great money-making opportunity in the long run.

Self-discipline helps transform pleasure-principle urges into reality-principle solutions. The investment counselor who makes exaggerated claims to lure clients might say to herself: "If I make realistic claims to prospective clients, I will lose out on a few quick commissions. Yet in the long term I'll make more money. I may start with a smaller client base, but I will build a loyal following because of my honesty." Enough pep talks to oneself of this nature will help create the right thought patterns to engage the reality principle, thus helping you avoid trouble.

SELF-DISCIPLINE HELPS TRANSFORM PLEASURE-PRINCIPLE URGES INTO REALITY-PRINCIPLE SOLUTIONS.

Wesley Snipes, the popular movie actor who plays in many action films, grew up in the South Bronx, where the temptation is strong for getting into legal and drug trouble. Snipes credits his mother, Marian, for helping him develop the self-discipline that has kept him focused and motivated and out of trouble. Marian was a teacher's aide in every South Bronx school attended by Snipes and his younger sister, Brigitte. "I feared the wrath of Marian. My mom was no joke. She still isn't. Whenever I got into a fight, she'd catch me in the stairwell, before I could even get to the dean's office. Sometimes she never said a word. I'd just hear the whoosh of her hand. Man, she had me locked up."

The discipline imposed by Snipes' mother gradually converted to self-discipline. Recognizing that staying out of trouble would help him in the long run, Snipes became a serious student. He seized the opportunity to act in school plays, assiduously memorizing his lines while many of his neighborhood pals were getting into trouble with the law. When one of his teachers recommended that he audition at the prestigious New York High School for Performing Arts, he did and was accepted. This was the foundation for his acting career.

APPLYING THE REALITY PRINCIPLE

The major implication of the reality principle is clear-cut: Delay immediate gratification of your impulses if it will prove more valuable in the long term. However, this pronouncement does not mean that immediate impulse gratification is never warranted. So what if you take off an occasional afternoon to play golf when you could have been getting more work accomplished? An infrequent deviation from a routine is refreshing. So what if you occasionally binge on Polish sausage or a hamburger? Any healthy person can eat high-fat food once in a while. So what if you have an impromptu romance with somebody you know will never become your significant other? With adequate precaution, it could prove to be the bridge to someone better.

When you are faced with decisions that present a conflict between your immediate and long-term interests and you need to reignite your reality principle, ask yourself the following questions:

1. Will instant gratification of my needs interfere with my long-term best interests?
2. Am I taking this action just to relieve some immediate pain rather than working out a sensible solution to my problem?
3. Which course of action will bring me the most net fun a year from now?
4. Should I avoid my instincts here if following them might get me into big trouble?

5. What is really important to me?

6. Is it worth enduring a little discomfort now, to enjoy a big comfort later?

Your answers to these questions will help you choose between instant gratification and long-range gain. Each has its place in your life. It's up to you to determine when and how.

THE PROCRASTINATION CONUNDRUM

In *Skin Deep*, a movie starring John Ritter, an alcoholic pleads with his psychiatrist to help him with his drinking problem. The psychiatrist responds, "I can't help you until you stop drinking." A similar Catch-22 situation occurs in the relationship between self-discipline and procrastination. Being a procrastinator blocks you from being self-disciplined, but to overcome procrastination, you must exercise considerable self-discipline.

Although this logic may appear circular, there is a sense to it. In fact, it has its parallel in the effort of overcoming a physical disability.

Imagine a tennis player who has torn a ligament in her leg—an injury so severe that she cannot run well enough to play tennis seriously. She can't even walk without limping. Her physical therapy treatment requires her to exercise, which includes light walking. And so, the cure for the problem of not being able to walk or run is to start walking and running. You can learn how to conquer procrastination and low self-discipline by using small doses of self-discipline.

In this chapter we will examine the causes of procrastination and how it can be brought under control. Conquering procrastination will be of enormous benefit to you. It will improve your success, lower your stress, and help you build a reputation of being a self-disciplined achiever. Without getting procrastination under control, you will never be highly self-disciplined.

HOW DO YOU KNOW WHEN YOU ARE PROCRASTINATING?

A clear sign of it is when you have no valid excuse for not getting projects and tasks accomplished. However, there are much more subtle signs. You are probably procrastinating if three or more of the following symptoms apply to you:

- You overorganize a project by such rituals as sharpening every pencil, meticulously straightening out your desk, reviewing all your third-class mail, and discarding bent paper clips.
- You keep waiting for the right time to do something, such as getting started on an important report.
- You are easily distracted, and have problems choosing between the important and the trivial.
- You underestimate the time needed to do a project, and say to yourself, "This won't take much time, so I can do it next week."

50

- You are often too tired to start or finish a project that needs doing.
- You trivialize a task by saying it's not worth doing.
- You spend more time hoping and wishing for good times to happen than taking steps to create happiness.
- Your goals are vague, such as "buying a luxury car," "losing weight," or "living a fabulous lifestyle."
- You have not developed action plans to achieve your goals.
- You are easily distracted and bored.

THE ROOTS OF PROCRASTINATION

To conquer procrastination, you have to understand the probable cause related to the action that is being delayed or postponed indefinitely. Then you need to take decisive action to get moving on the blocked task. For now, let's take a look at the eleven most frequent causes of procrastination; the cause often points toward the cure.

Moving Outside Your Comfort Zone

A comfort zone refers to an area of functioning in which you believe you can readily handle challenges. A major contributor to procrastination is being challenged to move out of your comfort zone by an unfamiliar or difficult task. Consider Jeff, an account executive at an advertising agency. He missed out on many potential networking opportunities because he procrastinated for years about learning golf. Because he fared much better in team sports, he felt golf was outside his comfort zone.

Most people feel nervous and insecure when facing a challenge outside their comfort zone.[1] And so, the automatic reaction is to avoid activities that evoke these feelings. Instead of rising to the challenge, we make up plausible excuses for not proceeding. Of course, each plausible excuse has a counterargument that could be made for going ahead with the new challenge—in other words, a way to exist outside the comfort zone. In Jeff's case, he might say, "Golf would be an investment in time and money but the payoff would be excellent. I will dramatically increase my business contacts."

Another situation that takes us outside the comfort zone—and leads us to procrastination—is facing overwhelming or tedious tasks. A business owner might want to delay preparing an employee pension report for the government because the task appears overwhelming and tedious. However, if she used self-discipline and became adept at preparing these reports, they would fall *within* her comfort zone, and she would be less likely to procrastinate.

Fear of Failure

Procrastination is often tied to fear of failure. For example, if you delay preparing a report for your boss, your boss cannot criticize its quality. Many professionals delay taking licensing or certifying exams because they are flat out afraid of not passing.

Fear of Success

Some people who fear success harbor the conviction that it will bring some unwelcome outcomes such as isolation and abandonment.[2] They worry that being successful will create envy and resentment among their colleagues. Others are concerned that expectations of them will rise. An industrial sales representative explained his fear of success in this way:

> I'm having an incredibly good year, and I'm worried about it. My sales were 36 percent above quota. Of course, I welcome the giant commission check I'll be receiving. But now my manager and the marketing vice president think I'm Superman. If I have an ordinary

sales year next year, the company will think I'm resting on my laurels. I would prefer my sales to creep up gradually, rather than have such a big surge.

Fear of Independence and Responsibility

You can put things off for so long that it brings on a real crisis from which you need to be rescued. Take, for example, Marie, who postponed preventive maintenance of her car so long that it required a new engine. Being unable to afford such a repair, she had to ask her parents for help.

Some college students procrastinate completing college because they fear being out on their own. As one undergraduate said, "I don't want to be out on my own at age 22. I would much prefer living in a dorm and getting by on checks from my parents."

Fear of Bad News Beyond Your Control

When a person fears that bad news is forthcoming, he might hesitate to follow through on the action that will uncover the bad news. For example, if you think you need root canal surgery, postponing a trip to the dentist will block you from receiving that unfavorable diagnosis. If you think a candid discussion with your manager will reveal that you might be included in the next round of layoffs, you might procrastinate scheduling a meeting on the topic.

Like most contributors to procrastination, fear of bad news can prevent you from taking the constructive action needed to deal with your problem. If you *do* have root canal disease, delaying a visit to the dentist will multiply your problem; and if you *don't* have root canal disease, delaying a visit to the dentist will only prolong needless fear and worry.

Perfectionism

Being a perfectionist is another potential contributor to procrastination. If you do not consider a project complete until it is perfect, you might seriously delay or fail to complete the project. Interestingly, computers have become partners in perfectionism. Modifying reports and graphics is so easy that it is tempting to continually prepare new drafts—and miss deadlines.

The total quality management movement contributes to procrastination stemming from perfectionism. If workers do not consider a project complete until no errors are detectable, they might procrastinate signing off on a project. To cope with this conflict, it is helpful to commit yourself to a goal such as, "I will search for defects on my project up until June 15. At that date it will be shipped, with as high quality as possible."

A lesser form of perfectionism is to be overcautious about your work. Success evangelist Napoleon Hill defined this symptom as:

> The habit of looking for the negative side of every circumstance, thinking and talking of possible failure instead of concentrating on the means of succeeding. Knowing all the roads to disaster, but never searching for the plans to avoid failure. Waiting for the right time to begin putting plans into action, until the waiting becomes a permanent habit. Remembering those who have failed, and forgetting those who have succeeded.[3]

The self-disciplined person will exercise appropriate caution but is focused enough to look for success opportunities. He thinks along these lines: "I know 100 things can go wrong, but it doesn't matter. If I don't commit myself to a course of action, I can never achieve what I want."

Apparent Lack of Meaningful Reward

People frequently put off doing tasks that don't appear to offer a meaningful reward. Suppose you decided that your computer files need a thorough updating, including deleting inactive files. Even if you know it should be done, its accomplishment in and of itself is not enough of a reward. The highly self-disciplined person, however, will find a meaningful reward in almost any activity. In this situation, she will think: "If I update and delete my files, I'll be able to work with a clearer, fresher perspective. Getting rid of the clutter will enable my mind to be less distracted."

Rebelling Against Control

Many people procrastinate as a way of rebelling against being in control. Used in this way, procrastination is a means of defying unwanted authority.[4] Rather than submit to authority, the person might say silently, "Nobody is going to tell me when I should get a report done. I'll do it when I'm ready."

The person who uses procrastination to rebel against control faces a continuous struggle. Many deadlines are imposed on us by people with the authority to make our lives miserable if we don't comply. If you fail to renew your automobile license on time through the mail, you are forced to make an in-person visit to the motor vehicle bureau and take a new driver's exam. If you don't comply with federal government tax deadlines, you are forced to pay interest rates exceeding those charged by credit-card companies, department-store revolving charges, and loan sharks. If you are chronically late with job assignments, you can be zapped with poor performance appraisals and dismissal.

Cop-out for Poor Performance

Procrastinators suffer a continuous time crunch because they fritter away so much time. They never seem to have enough time to start, implement, or complete a task. The procrastinator's constant refrain is, "If I only had more time, I could have done a great job."[5] Lack of sufficient time to do a task properly then becomes a good excuse for poor performance. In the procrastinator's way of thinking, she cannot be fully blamed for what went wrong—the real villain is lack of time!

You will recall from the self-discipline model that the self-disciplined person minimizes excuse making. Lack of time is not needed as a lame excuse because the self-disciplined person creates time for important tasks.

Negative Stimulation and Excitement

A curious reason for procrastination is to achieve the stimulation and excitement that stems from rushing to meet a deadline.[6] The process works this way: You have an 11:00 a.m. appointment on the other side of town. The appointment should comfortably take about 50 minutes to reach by car. You delay getting your papers and notes together for the meeting until 9:30. As luck would have it, you can't locate what you need. You frantically race through papers on your desk. Finally, at 10:10 you rush out of the office and get into your car at 10:15.

Fearing that you will be late you squeeze through amber lights. You blast your horn at senior citizens in front of you who are driving under the speed limit. You rifle through your glove compartment for a city map because you are not certain where to get off the expressway. You attempt to read the map at a red light. You make a quick call on your cellular telephone to advise your appointment that you are running 10 minutes behind schedule.

Your adrenaline is pumping; you are swearing at yourself. Yet you really like it that way. You need your daily fix of negative stress. Admit it, you enjoy getting high on your hormones. If you had not procrastinated getting ready for this appointment you would have had a well-planned, calm, boring morning. That's why you did not prepare for your appointment earlier in the morning or the night before.

Self-Defeating Behavior

I have saved the mother of all causes of procrastination for last. A deep-rooted reason for procrastination is a conscious or unconscious attempt to bring about personal failure. For example, a person might be recommended for an almost ideal job opportunity, yet he delays sending a resume for so long that the potential employer loses interest.

Self-defeating behavior is closely related to the other reasons for procrastination. For instance, a person who fears success may engage in self-defeating behavior to block success. Rather than perform admirably during a command performance, the person may mess up hoping that she will be excluded from additional demanding assignments.

Despite these multiple causes of procrastination, many constructive steps can be taken to cope with the problem and get back on track toward being self-disciplined.

USING THE SELF-DISCIPLINE MODEL TO CONQUER PROCRASTINATION

Until you can control procrastination you will never be a self-disciplined achiever. A comprehensive approach to conquering procrastination is applying the self-discipline model presented in Chapter 1. Applying the model begins by *formulating your mission statement*. A well-articulated mission statement should give you a compelling purpose for accomplishing important feats. The purpose gives you the emotional lift to help overcome temptations to procrastinate. A person whose mission is to become a well-respected leader in his field is less likely to procrastinate about learning new technology to help him achieve his mission.

Role models are useful in helping you conquer procrastination. Search for a successful person in your network who rarely procrastinates. Ask that person how she gets so many things done on time. Charlene, an information systems specialist with a procrastination problem, asked her manager how she seems to get everything done despite her many competing demands. The manager responded, "I circle in red the most important items on my to-do list each day. In my mind, not getting those items done is a criminal act perpetrated against myself or others. If I have to work from after dinner until midnight to complete a task, I will. Fortunately for my family, I usually get my work done before 6:00 in the evening."

The next step in the model is to *develop goals for each task*. In dealing with a specific task that you are liable to procrastinate, establish antiprocrastination goals, however humble. Knocking off the little goals will give you the momentum to accomplish the bigger ones. If you are concerned that you will procrastinate staining your new backyard fence, begin with a modest goal such as, "By March 15, I will buy the stain and brushes," or "On March 22, I will apply the stain from 12:30 until 2:00." If you are planning a second career but have been procrastinating taking any constructive action for four years, start with a small goal such as, "On September 1, I will call to order a ticket for the franchise exhibition coming to town in October."

Now you're ready to *develop action plans to achieve goals*. Incorporate a few of the more appealing procrastination antidotes into your daily life. You might decide, for example, to subdivide a large project into small chunks. You then invest 20 minutes per day for five days to begin chipping away at this overwhelming task.

You can also use *visual and sensory stimulation* to help you in your struggle with procrastination. Imagine what it would be like to be on top of every project and task in your in-basket or listed in your e-mail. Imagine going home from work and saying to yourself, "I am right on target with all my assignments this month. I just need to do 30 minutes of paperwork this evening, then I can devote my full attention to the family." Visualize yourself being on schedule with such personal life tasks as having your auto serviced, your furnace tuned, your dry cleaning already back from the cleaners, and your checkbook balanced. You could then say to yourself, "I can concentrate better on my work at the office because my mind is clear. My household chores are under control."

Visualize how good you would feel if superiors, coworkers, subordinates, and family members were not badgering you with questions like, "By any chance have you contacted our Japanese affiliate yet about the price increases?" or "When are you going to pay the orthodontist so Kim can get her treatments started?"

Moving to the next step in the model, you can also combat procrastination if you *search for the pleasure within the task.* Given that a major reason for procrastination is that a specific task seems so overwhelmingly miserable, you may have to dig harder to find the intrinsic rewards. Consider Sam, who has to make a presentation to management defending why his department should not be downsized. He typically doesn't like making presentations to management, and this presentation is an assignment from hell. To get through this, he identifies something within the presentation itself that is pleasurable. Since he enjoys collating facts and figures and preparing computer graphics, he focuses on those activities, which give him enough momentum to get the project rolling.

IF PROCRASTINATION WERE STRICTLY A TIME-MANAGEMENT PROBLEM, A PROCRASTINATOR COULD SIMPLY PREPARE A TO-DO LIST, PRIORITIZE THE ITEMS, AND GET TO WORK.

You can also make some progress against procrastination if you *compartmentalize spheres of life.* Part of the reason you are delaying a project might be that the multiple demands on your time seem so overwhelming. Mentally wear the same blinders placed on horses so they can concentrate better on the race and not be distracted. Say to yourself, "I'm devoting tonight exclusively to one giant task—collecting the necessary information for my tax returns. I will therefore forget about work, television, and romance from 7:00 until 10:00."

Compartmentalizing is a powerful way to attack procrastination because it focuses your efforts on one sphere of life at a time. Do you recall how easy it is to not procrastinate when you have very little to do? You simply energize your efforts to concentrate on one or two small items facing you. Procrastination is more tempting when multiple demands are swirling and competing in your mind.

Finally, procrastination will decrease dramatically if you minimize excuse making. A person who has been delaying exercising for five years might say to himself: "For five years I've been making up feeble excuses for not getting my body into shape. The year my father died, my excuse was that I just couldn't get into worrying about myself. Another year, I changed jobs so I couldn't concentrate on exercising. Then one year, I was struggling with migraines, so I couldn't do much of anything.

"Starting three minutes from now, the delays are over. I'm going to do one complete push-up if I squirm for 15 minutes like a turtle on its back. Maybe within two months I'll be doing 15 push-ups. But that's the future. My muscle toning regimen is now only two minutes and 30 seconds away. OK, now down to the floor with my body."

A VARIETY OF WAYS TO ATTACK THE PROCRASTINATION PROBLEM

In addition to applying the self-discipline model to conquering procrastination, you can also capitalize on a wide variety of other techniques, which are described below. All of them are compatible with the model and can be incorporated into the self-discipline model as action plans.

You won't need to use every technique described here for overcoming a procrastination problem. A more realistic approach is to pick and choose among the techniques for those that are best suited to your situation.

DEALING WITH MENTAL ATTITUDES AND PERCEPTIONS

If procrastination were strictly a time-management problem, a procrastinator could simply prepare a to-do list, prioritize the items, and get to work. In reality, procrastination involves a host of mental attitudes and perceptions that lead to serious delays in getting tasks accomplished on time or even doing them at all. The most serious cases of procrastination may be symptoms of emotional conflict that require the assistance of a mental health professional. Here are some winning tactics for overcoming procrastination that should work for anyone whose procrastination is not pathological.

Watch Out for Early-Warning Signals

Time-management consultant Dru Scott recommends that people be alert to how they procrastinate. If you stay alert to these early-warning signals, you should be able to mobilize an appropriate antidote to procrastination. Here are several common signals[7]:

- When you have mixed emotions about a project, do you suddenly become fatigued?
- When you are facing a big task, do you suddenly get so hungry that you have to delay action until you have gone out for a snack?
- Do you begin straightening your desk when it is time to get started on a new project?
- When faced with a demanding chore, do you suddenly decide it's time to make a luncheon appointment with several key people in your network?

61

At times the above rituals can be healthy. For example, straightening out your desk is a good idea because it helps you clear your mind and gives you a fresh perspective. However, if the purpose of desk-clearing is to avoid action, then you know your procrastination cycle has begun.

Recognize You Have Time to Do Things You Want

Almost all procrastinators are able to promptly take care of selected tasks they enjoy doing. Many procrastinators, in general, do find the time to collect their paycheck, demand a raise, go bowling, or send away for tickets to athletic or music events. Identify those activities you rarely procrastinate. After forming this mental image, ask yourself why you have been unable to use the same self-discipline to accomplish the activity you have been avoiding. You may find that you can create the space to take care of the activity you have been delaying for no valid reason.

Write Down What Might Be Blocking You

Self-analysis can often help you determine the real problem blocking you from getting started on an activity. Beverly said to her husband Jason, "I've heard from three friends at work that marriage enrichment weekends are great at re-energizing relationships. I think that we should go to one. It doesn't cost much, and I think we'd both enjoy it." Jason unenthusiastically agreed to attend, saying, "It's alright with me. Make the arrangements, and let me know."

Beverly was happy that Jason said yes, yet she placed the brochure in her desk drawer and took no action. At the prompting of a friend who was a school psychologist, the woman prepared a list of why she thought she was blocking on making final arrangements. Her list included these entries: (1) "I think Jason is just humoring me. He really doesn't want to attend, so we wouldn't get much out of it." (2) "If the weekend involves some heavy sessions, we might reveal some real flaws in our relationship. That would hurt the closeness we now have." (3) "We both might find that some of the other couples are happier than we are. That would be very discouraging."

It became apparent to Beverly that the reasons she was procrastinating were sensible, yet she still thought that the weekend would benefit her marriage. Her solution was to discuss her reservations and concerns with Jason. He said nothing strangers could say would hurt their marriage. With her concerns alleviated, Beverly made reservations for what proved to be an enriching experience.

Calculate the Cost of Procrastination

You can reduce procrastination by calculating its cost. For example, you might lose out on a high-paying job you really want by not having your resume and cover letter ready. Your cost of procrastination would include the difference between the job you find and the one you really want. The cost of procrastination for delaying putting two quarts of oil in your engine could be $3,500 to replace a seized engine. (But subtract from that figure the $1.75 you saved by not buying the oil.) The cost of procrastination for Beverly and Jason would be a less-enriched marriage.

Reward and Punish Yourself As Appropriate

A standard procrastination antidote is to self-administer rewards and punishments to modify your behavior in the right direction. Give yourself a pleasant reward soon after accomplishing an unpleasant task. Remember Sam, who was delaying preparing a presentation justifying his group's existence? If he did finish the report, he might buy himself a luxury fountain pen. Of course, if his presentation were effective his reward would be a saved job.

The second part of the tactic is to punish yourself with something you despise after you discover you have been procrastinating. Suppose you have procrastinated getting a birthday present for a close friend. How about finding all the empty bottles and cans around your home and returning them to the supermarket during a beautiful Saturday afternoon?

Make a Commitment to Other People

Make it imperative that you get something done on time by making a commitment to other people. You might announce to coworkers that you are going to get something accomplished by a certain date. If you fail to meet this date, you are likely to feel embarrassed. In this way you are capitalizing on the power of self-punishment.

YOUR FEARS ARE ONLY VALID IN TERMS OF THEIR CONSEQUENCES.

Making a commitment to other people, as to any other single technique for overcoming procrastination, does not always work. How many people have you heard in recent years proclaim on January 1, "This is my year, I'm finally going to lose ten pounds (or start saving money, or stop smoking, or stop drinking, or stop chewing gum)"? It is best to combine several methods in an assault on procrastination.

Imagine the Worst Consequences

A widely used technique to overcome worries involves asking oneself, "What is the worst thing that could happen if I did _____?" You can use the same technique to overcome procrastination.[9] The underlying problem is that our imagination often distorts our fears to unreasonable proportions, and we may begin to dread consequences that have yet to take place or may never take place. You might dread telling your boss that you are quitting for fear of being perceived as an ingrate, and

64

ruining a work relationship. You therefore procrastinate making the announcement, even though your day of departure is approaching rapidly.

To prevent unreasonable fear from creating procrastination, proceed as follows: Write down the worst possible outcome that could happen if you carried out the activity you are avoiding. Would you be embarrassed? Would you be humiliated? Would you be treated rudely? Would you be rejected forever? Would the other person say "no"? Would the other person say "yes"? Would you be impoverished?

The activity that I fear:

_____

_____

_____

The worst thing that could happen:

_____

_____

_____

After you have made your entries, read each item out loud. Laugh at yourself when warranted. You will see that some of the consequences of your fears are not consequential. So what if your boss is unhappy that you are quitting? Most employers have little concern about dismissing people. Leaving a company for a better opportunity is certainly not deviant behavior.

The "worst consequences" activity is helpful in sorting out legitimate versus illegitimate fears. In the majority of instances, the worst possible consequences of carrying out an activity are not so severe that procrastination is warranted. You are likely to recognize that the negative consequences from procrastinating are more damaging than the worst consequences from action. For example, the worst consequences from getting a copy of your credit rating is that you could learn that you have a few trouble spots in your credit history. The worst consequences from procrastinating getting a copy of the report is that you do not take action on your credit problems. You might not be able to obtain a large loan when you need one.

Change from the Critic to Doer Mode

Self-help guru Wayne W. Dyer believes that some people procrastinate because criticizing rather than doing has become a major theme in their life.[10] Instead of accomplishing activities, the critic enjoys belittling the efforts of others. Rather than taking the initiative to suggest methods of saving money for the company, the critic pokes fun at the suggestions of others. It is understandable why many people prefer to criticize than to do: criticism is easier than action. Quite often the sports fan who hurls the worst insults at the athletes on the field is a person who has never competed athletically.

Constructive criticism is important, yet people who invest too much time in criticizing others may fail to grow. Critics postpone activities of their own because they are so involved in criticism.

To overcome procrastination stemming from being a critic instead of a doer, first recognize any tendency in this direction you might have. Recognize that some people criticize others because they are projecting their own shortcomings onto others. Resolve to start creating accomplishments of your own rather than settling for occupying the role of full-time critic.

Satisfy Your Stimulation Quota In Constructive Ways

If you procrastinate because you enjoy the rush of scrambling to make deadlines, find a more constructive way of using busyness to keep you humming. If you need a high level of stimulation, enrich your life with extra projects, learning new skills, and volunteering for activities that could make an impact on your company if carried out successfully. The fullness of your schedule will provide you the stimulation you had been receiving from squeezing yourself to make deadlines and reach appointments on time.[11]

Program Your Brain Not to Procrastinate

As psychotechnology continues to advance, ways are developing for programming your brain not to procrastinate. The simplest technique is to place notes around your home and work environment with messages such as, "Get It Done," "Do It Now," or simply "Do It." (Thank you Nike for the last message.) Constant reminders of such a message can become a form of mental programming.

Another approach to programming your brain can be accomplished with high technology. Software called Mindset flashes reinforcing messages across the menu bar on your computer screen. You can adjust the frequency and duration of the suggestions. The message can flash by subliminally (below the level of conscious awareness). Or it can remain on the screen for several seconds. The procrastination message is: "My goals are obtainable. I am confident in my abilities. I make and keep deadlines."[12]

The brain can also be programmed during its sleeping state by going to sleep with positively stated questions.[13] Here are a few samples:

- "How can I get this project completed on time and in a high-quality manner?"
- "How can I get my taxes done on time to avoid paying penalties?"
- "How can I conduct all seven performance appraisals by the end of the year and still get my budget report in on time?"

Brain programming to overcome procrastination works better for some people than others. I suspect people who are more suggestible (and therefore more readily hypnotized) respond best to programming. The technique is certainly worth a try because the effort and expense are so modest.

DEAL WITH THE TASK ITSELF

In addition to modifying your attitudes and perceptions in relation to procrastination, you can also benefit from attacking the task itself. Modifying the task might then lead to an attitude change, particularly when the task becomes less threatening. Here are some time-tested tactics for dealing directly with the task you are delaying:

- *Break the task into manageable chunks.* A major contributor to procrastination is a task that seems overwhelming. The solution is to divide the project into small projects that seem less formidable. You may have heard this approach called the elephant technique. This technique is based on the straightforward idea that eating an entire elephant in one sitting would be more than anyone could handle. A more sensible approach would be to eat the elephant one bite at a time.

  Breaking a task into manageable chunks works best when you have ample time to work on a project, enabling you to give it part-time attention. For example, you might work on your income tax return over three months, instead of three nights. The technique also is useful on a project requiring full-time attention. If your job calls for inspecting 20 locations within 30 days, begin by scheduling inspections of the two closest to home. Then gradually work your way further out.

  How does this technique for overcoming procrastination relate to self-discipline? By using the mechanical aid of breaking a task into subcomponents, it becomes easier for you to focus on your goal and take action. And focusing on a goal and taking action are core behaviors of the self-disciplined achiever.

- *Choose a designated time slot for the procrastinated task.* The best quick-fix technique for getting moving on a procrastinated task is to decide when you will get started. By choosing a designated time slot, you have taken your first bite of the elephant. Suppose you've been asked to organize a teleconference for a new product introduction. Since your company is new to teleconferencing, you do not have access to a teleconferencing specialist who will take care of all the technical arrangements. Instead, it will be your responsibility to uncover how such a teleconference can be arranged. Placed on top of all your other responsibilities, the teleconferencing assignment seems overwhelming.

  Suppose also that you are responding to this request very slowly. You have placed making the arrangements on your to-do list, but not much is happening. After one week has passed, you admit to yourself that you are procrastinating. You can ease the pain of getting started by designating 30 minutes (perhaps Friday from 11:30 till noon) as Day One of the project. You commit yourself to making a few preliminary phone calls or faxing inquiries to teleconferencing studios. Or perhaps you will call somebody in your network who might know something about teleconferencing.

- *Create some momentum to get you moving.* A way to get momentum going is to find a leading task to perform; that is, an easy, warmup activity that consumes very little time. If you have delayed starting a physical fitness campaign for yourself, you might begin by listing a few easy, warmup activities such as: cleaning out a drawer for your athletic attire, purchasing a spiral notebook to keep a log of your fitness activities, going for a walk around the block after dinner this evening, or doing three sit-ups as soon as you finish reading this chapter.

The leading-task technique works equally well in the office. For instance, if you are procrastinating conducting an audit, you might begin by finding a file for the project.

Discover Your Peak Activation Time

Most people have energy cycles governing both their physical and mental energy. Reflect back carefully as to which time of the day you are usually at your peak productivity and creativity. For most of us it occurs within two hours after waking. If you are not sure of this peak activation period for you, observe your behavior during the next two weeks.

You can use your peak activation time as the designated time slot for *demanding* work on the project you are procrastinating, for instance a strategic plan, because it requires creativity and vision. You will appear highly self-disciplined—and be self-disciplined—if you work on creative tasks when you're at the peak of mental efficiency.

Take Power Naps to Recharge

You certainly don't need a high degree of self-discipline to take 10- to 15-minute naps! The purpose of the nap is to gradually develop your self-discipline by attacking procrastinated chores immediately after the nap. The power nap is so labeled because a brief nap gives you a surge of power much more effective than caffeine or sweets.

Schedule a nap during a time at which you are most likely to feel woozy. For most, this occurs at three in the afternoon. But you'd better set an alarm clock or radio to prevent the power nap from extending to an afternoon's sleep. Plan which task you are going to work on following the nap for about 30 minutes.

For those who work at home, where to find a power nap is not a problem. People with private offices can also find a place to nap. If you don't have an office, you'll need to improvise. In moderate climates, your car will suffice. Or, find a deserted store room.

Keep in mind what you are trying to accomplish by using these antidotes to procrastination. Until you overcome procrastination, you will never be self-disciplined. Yet you will need to use a modicum of self-discipline to help you get the success cycle going: A little self-discipline will help you start to overcome procrastination, which will lead to more self-discipline, and less and less procrastination.

THE SYMBIOTIC RELATIONSHIP BETWEEN SELF-LEADERSHIP & SELF-DISCIPLINE

The new trim workplace is demanding more and more from employees. For instance, to elicit a higher level of problem solving and creativity, managers are asking them to be more self-directing. A positive outcome of this is an empowered workforce comprising people who can work independently at a high level of competence.

To be a successful member of the new workplace, you must exercise self-leadership—which is a process of influencing oneself to accomplish important and complex purposes. The self-led person is the opposite of the heel dragger who requires constant external rewards and threats of punishment to sustain effort. Self-leadership is essential to such activities as launching a new product or completing a divisional strategic plan on time and without supervision.

Self-discipline and self-leadership go hand in hand. The self-disciplined person stays focused on an important goal until it is achieved. A person who exercises self-leadership influences herself to achieve worthwhile objectives. If you are self-disciplined it is easier to exercise self-leadership. And if you learn how to lead yourself, it will be easier to exercise self-discipline. Self-discipline and self-leadership thus have a symbiotic, mutually beneficial, relationship.

If you practice true self-leadership you are a joy to your boss and the company. Your manager doesn't have to figure out how to inspire you to achieve high performance; instead he can concentrate on high-level problem solving and working with those who are dependent on others for leadership.

Exercising self-leadership and empowering yourself also pay giant dividends in personal life. Instead of waiting for others to tell you what to do, how to run your life, or whether it is time to explore investments, you forge new paths for yourself.

To get started thinking seriously about developing self-leadership and personal empowerment, I'd like you to take the quiz on page 74.

> YOU CAN DIRECT YOUR ENERGY TOWARD IMPORTANT GOALS AND EMPOWER YOURSELF TO TAKE ON IMPORTANT RESPONSIBILITIES WITHOUT WAITING FOR OTHERS TO MOTIVATE YOU.

EMPOWERED ACTIONS IN WORK AND PERSONAL LIFE

Self-leadership and empowerment are characteristics you can find in people from the shop floor to the executive suite. As a result,

(text continues on page 76)

THE SELF-LEADERSHIP AND PERSONAL EMPOWERMENT QUIZ

Indicate the extent of your agreement with the following statements using the following scale and circling the numbers below: disagree strongly (DS); disagree (D); neutral (N); agree (A); and, agree strongly (AS). Circle the number under the answer that best fits your attitude.

	DS	D	N	A	AS
1. I work best when I have a detailed and unambiguous job description.	5	4	3	2	1
2. I prefer to consult with my manager before taking action when I face a controversy.	5	4	3	2	1
3. My managers have had relatively little impact on my work performance.	1	2	3	4	5
4. Over the years I've been assertive about making new friends.	1	2	3	4	5
5. I feel there's very little a person can do to improve neighborhood problems.	5	4	3	2	1
6. After someone tells me what he or she wants me to accomplish, I much prefer figuring out how to get the task accomplished.	1	2	3	4	5
7. I would enjoy working for someone I saw only three times a year.	1	2	3	4	5

quiz continues

	DS	D	N	A	AS
8. Unless a person holds an executive position, there is very little he or she can do to make a difference in a company.	5	4	3	2	1
9. I chart my own direction in life.	1	2	3	4	5
10. I typically ask permission before doing any activity out of the ordinary.	5	4	3	2	1

Scoring and Interpretation

Add the sum of the numbers you have circled. Interpret your score as follows:

40–50 points:

Your attitudes are strongly in the direction of a self-leader who looks to empower himself or herself.

30–39 points:

You have a moderate tendency toward being a self-leader and one who empowers himself or herself.

10–29 points:

Your attitudes are those of a person who depends on others for leadership and empowerment. Study the ideas in this chapter carefully and implement some of them if you are interested in becoming more self-directing.

production workers are being empowered to assume such responsibilities as implementing process improvements and working with external suppliers and customers. Retail workers are being empowered to handle substantial customer problems without consulting the store manager. And managers, professionals, and salespeople are also being empowered to assume more responsibility—often because of downsizing.

Rick, a regional manager in an office products company, made this observation:

> Up until two years ago we had six regional managers. We now have two, and I'm one of them. This means I'm doing the work formerly done by three regional managers. We did get rid of many meetings and reports, which has helped reduce the workload, yet I still have a lot more responsibility than before.
>
> I'm working longer hours but I enjoy the extra responsibility. I feel more like a real regional manager because top management lets me run my own show more than they did in the past. Part of the reason is that I'm handling so many things that it's too confusing to check in with corporate headquarters on everything. My budget responsibility alone has doubled.

Self-leadership is not just a nine-to-five activity. You can direct your energy toward important personal goals and empower yourself to assume responsibilities without waiting for others—family, friends—to motivate you. Here's a sampling of self-leadership and personal empowerment activities off the job that people have shared with me:

- I was tired of paying so many bills every month, so I decided to make double payments, thus reducing my monthly paperwork. Now when I receive a bill, it shows a credit in my favor. More important, I also have more time to invest in pursuits more rewarding than bill paying.

- I was approached by the United Way for my yearly contribution. But this year, I decided to experiment with direct charity. I "adopted" a needy family and give them monthly contributions equal to the money I paid United Way. I feel great because I'm directly helping a family, and I can see the smiles on their faces.

- I've appointed myself the OSHA (Occupational Safety and Health Act) official at home. I make notes of all the unsafe and unhealthy conditions in the house. The violations I detected include: (1) house too tightly sealed, leading to unhealthy air despite a small cost savings in fuel, (2) a loose step on the stairs for the back deck, (3) four pairs of boots and old tennis shoes with treads so smooth, slipping on wet pavement is almost inevitable, and (4) five bottles of medicine with expiration dates of five or more years old. A family conference leads to action plans for remedying all these unsafe and unhealthy conditions.

A PERSON WITH A WHEELBARROW PERSONALITY IS USELESS UNLESS LOADED, POINTED, AND PUSHED BY SOMEONE ELSE.

- My sex life with my spouse of 25 years was losing its lustre. But, instead of grumbling and suffering in silence, I bought a video on sex-life enhancement narrated by a reputable sexologist. Then one night I lit some candles, opened a bottle of champagne, and turned on the video. The first night's results show a good return on investment—we both feel empowered!

DEVELOPING INITIATIVE

Charles R. McConnell, a health-care administrator, tells the story of a young man who was preparing to take a self-study course designed to improve initiative.[1] The man acquired the proper books and audiotapes and assembled his supplies. Then he spent a month waiting for his superiors to tell him to get started, exhibiting what has been referred to as a *wheelbarrow personality*— useless unless loaded, pointed, and pushed by someone else.

Getting started working without external prodding is but one manifestation of initiative. Another is to identify problems that need solving. A creative and self-disciplined person scans the environment to see what problems require resolution. On the job, problem finding can include such activities as:

- Spotting quality problems before customers do, thus preventing returns and ill will.
- Observing when a team member is having trouble learning a task properly and intervening before he commits a costly blooper.
- Identifying a project your team can undertake so it won't run out of work and face downsizing.
- Identifying work that contractors are performing that your team could do for less cost, and so enhance its contribution to the company.
- Identifying opportunities that your company is not yet exploring that would fit its capabilities, such as identifying products for the fastest-growing age group—people over 85.

Look for the initiative-taking opportunities in each situation. Whether you are in a meeting at work or having breakfast at home, ask yourself questions such as: "What could be improved upon here?" "What can I do that would make the team more satisfied and productive?" "What's missing from this situation that would make a contribution if it were present?" "What would my spouse like to happen that isn't happening?"

Finally, in any situation in which you have even a few discretionary minutes, ask yourself, "How can I make a bigger contribution?" Many people in large organizations deify job descriptions. According to their logic, their detailed job descriptions are etched in stone. Even the CEO has a tightly drawn list of responsibilities. Following your job description too closely, however, has a downside. You will fail to carry out activities not specified—and begin limiting possibilities and opportunities. Instead, empower yourself to look for ways to contribute more broadly than your job description requires. Many successful people routinely assume some of their manager's responsibility without being asked.

> Sue, a dental hygienist, noticed that her boss's dental practice was at a plateau. She thought to herself, "What else can I do to drum up more business for our office?" With her boss's approval, she started a fun-filled newsletter about dental care, aimed at parents and children. They mailed it to all current and former patients, as well as to a random selection of families within the area. The newsletter worked—the patient load increased a healthy 7 percent.

Up to this point, I have described examples of empowered actions and the importance of initiative. Developing self-leadership and empowerment, however, involves other mental processes: positive self-talk and controlling thinking.

SELF-LEADERSHIP AND POSITIVE SELF-TALK

One of the most important findings of psychological research during the past fifteen years is that positive self-talk influences performance. If you covertly tell yourself you will perform well on a complex mental or physical task, you increase your chances of performing well. Dozens of experiments with athletes and people with counterproductive habits have demonstrated that you can talk yourself into achieving your goals. One study even found that writer's block could be overcome to some extent if the writer gave himself pep talks.[2] (For example, "By 4:30 p.m. I will have the first draft of this technical report out of my printer and into the hands of my boss.")

Positive self-talk also contributes substantially to helping a person develop self-leadership. You can enhance your ability to influence yourself by making positive statements about your capabilities, such as "I know I can take charge of myself and achieve what I want" or "I can get my work done today without relying on help from my boss."

Positive self-talking may involve changing old habits and developing new ones by reprogramming the mental set, attitude, or belief that supports the outcome you want to change. I recommend the system of positive self-talk developed by Herb Kindler at the Center for Management Effectiveness in Pacific Palisades, California. The system centers around six key steps:[3]

1. Decide *specifically* what you want to do better to increase your effectiveness, satisfaction, or growth. In this instance you want to exercise self-leadership, thus being more dependent on yourself for direction and less dependent on others.

2. Affirm that the desired behavior is *already happening*. Use the *present* tense. "If you say, I *will* become a self-leader and become the prime mover of my own activities," the result is placed in the future, where it may remain beyond your immediate grasp. Instead, use the positive self-affirmation, "I am a self-leader and the prime mover of my own activities." You might also say, "I am empowering myself to carry out activities that are within my ability to achieve."

3. Include your *feelings* as part of your affirmation. You might say, "I'm thrilled about being able to get important tasks accomplished without depending on others to inspire or

cajole me." Another example is, "I'm happy that I have granted myself the authority to find happiness in a personal relationship."

4. Affirm the *positive*. Instead of saying, "I'm no longer going to mope around waiting for somebody else to motivate me," say, "I am a self-motivator. I rev myself up to get important tasks accomplished."

5. Affirm only what you believe truly is possible. Positive self-affirmations work best with accomplishments that your natural talents and acquired skills will allow. If you are 40 years old and have never learned to swim, you are not going to make the Olympic swim team of your country, despite your positive self-talk. Nevertheless, your positive self-talk can prompt you to acquire skills for which you have sufficient aptitude. Joan, for example, thought she could never do well enough on the GRE to be accepted into graduate school. Yet, she convinced herself to take the brush-up math and language courses to achieve the scores necessary for admittance to graduate school. The result? She achieved her demanding goal of being accepted.

6. Affirm only *your own behavior*, not the behavior of others. As you change, you will also influence how others react to you. Affirm that you are now more self-directing. This is better than affirming that others should grant you more freedom so you can exercise more self-leadership.

When you implement your program of self-affirmations[4] it is important to write down your affirmations and review them at least twice each week. Stay with the weekly reviews until you achieve the results you intended. Also, remember to use visual and sensory stimulation. As you look at each affirmation in a note-book, index card, or on a computer screen, visualize yourself experiencing the result you want:

It's 8:30 in the morning, and I'm in charge of my schedule. I'll figure out what needs to be done to achieve high productivity today. I see others scurrying to leave the office early because tomorrow is the start of a three-day weekend. I won't let this distract me from achieving my goals for the day. When I leave, I'll feel content knowing that I am in the right frame of mind to take a weekend vacation.

Most important, strive to have fun with your affirmations. Self-growth, self-discipline, and self-leadership are positive, life-enhancing experiences. It's fun, not drudgery, to know that you are the primary motivating force in your own life.

SELF-LEADERSHIP THROUGH CONTROLLING YOUR THINKING

A powerful approach for exercising self-leadership is to control your thinking so you can find the natural rewards in situations. (Similarly, the self-discipline model requires you to search for pleasure within a task. Again, self-discipline and self-leadership work symbiotically.) By making your cognitions more effective, you make situations self-rewarding. A key starting point is to understand the three primary features of naturally rewarding activities:[5] competence, control, and purpose.

Feelings of Competence

Naturally rewarding activities usually make us feel competent. If you perform well in an activity, such as dancing or putting together computer animations, you usually not only enjoy that activity, you also feel competent. The more you succeed with a task, the more you enjoy it. In turn, the more you enjoy a task, the more you will practice it and the more you will succeed.

Feelings of Self-Control

Naturally rewarding activities frequently make us feel more in control of our own activities. Setting your own schedule and choosing your own methods of work are key approaches to feeling in control. If you can arrange your work so you have control over when and how you do it, you'll feel more in control, and better able to exercise self-leadership. For many professional people, working at home at least one day a week facilitates a feeling of self-control over work.

Feelings of Purpose

Naturally rewarding activities also provide us with a sense of purpose. As Charles C. Manz, the premier authority in self-leadership observes, "Even if a task makes us feel more competent and more self-controlling, we still may have a difficult time naturally enjoying and being motivated by it if we do not believe in its worthiness."[6]

> SELF-GROWTH, SELF-DISCIPLINE, AND SELF-LEADERSHIP ARE POSITIVE, LIFE-ENHANCING EXPERIENCES.

Worthiness, social relevance, and meaningfulness are subjective and tied in with personal values. For instance, Walter and Jeanine work for a financial services firm specializing in underwriting and selling municipal bonds. Jeanine feels her work has no sense of purpose. Her perception of the nature of her job is as follows:

> I basically dislike what I'm doing. I'm helping the owners make a fortune, but I'm not really doing any social good. I'm just shuffling paper and making it possible for people in high tax brackets to earn tax-free income. I would be happier as a social worker.

Walter, however, perceives his job quite differently:

> I'm contributing to one of the most worthwhile financial undertakings in this country. Without municipal bonds, municipalities would have no money to build schools, roads, bridges, and

parks. Besides that, I'm helping thousands of people make investments that can secure their future.

The exercise on page 85 will help you discover your natural rewards.

Up to this point I have described the contribution of natural rewards to self-leadership. How can you capitalize on these natural rewards so you can achieve self-leadership? First, by building more naturally enjoyable features into activities, and second, focusing your thoughts on the naturally rewarding components of your activities.

Building Natural Rewards into Activities

Even if not every activity is a natural joy, you can often build enjoyable components into them. Suppose one of the natural motivators for you is to use computers on the job, yet your job does not involve full-time use of computers. To make your work activities more naturally motivating, computerize as much of your job as possible. If you are in sales, dream up as many applications for your laptop computer as possible: talk to your customers about forming electronic links between your computers; create a database of personal and social facts about your customers or clients.

A client of mine who is interested in photography learned how to make many activities of average motivational value into self-motivating situations through her hobby. For instance, one weekend Irene had to attend her niece's soccer game, even though she wasn't really interested in the sport. To make the game interesting, she took her camera with her and took action shots of the girls playing soccer, which not only stretched her skills but added excitement to the day. Irene also used her love of photography to get through a weekend business retreat. Although she found the agenda mildly stimulating, the idea of the retreat

EXERCISE FOR DISCOVERING YOUR NATURAL REWARDS[7]

To identify your naturally rewarding tasks, do the following analysis. You may need to observe your job activities over a couple of weeks in order to complete it.

1. List some of the activities that you naturally enjoy doing; where the incentive for doing the task is built into it.

   _____

   _____

   _____

2. Classify these activities and expand your list by identifying activities that provide you with a sense of:

   a. Competence _____

   _____

   _____

   b. Self-control _____

   _____

   _____

   c. Purpose _____

   _____

   _____

3. Identify activities that accomplish all three (provide you with a sense of competence, self-control, and purpose).

   _____

   _____

   _____

Source: Adapted from Charles C. Manz, _Mastering Self-Leadership: Empowering Yourself for Personal Excellence_ (Englewood Cliffs, NJ: Prentice Hall, 1992), p. 53.

left her flat. But she decided to empower herself to be the retreat photographer, which made the weekend more than just palatable. She gained a feeling of *competence* by operating a sophisticated still camera and doing a professional job of operating a camcorder; a feeling of *control* from deciding which photos to shoot, when to shoot them, and how; and a sense of purpose, because she was contributing to a pictorial history of her firm.

Focusing Your Thinking on the Natural Rewards

A self-led, self-disciplined achiever focuses on the natural motivators in the task, not the unpleasant aspects. If you think hard enough about the pleasant aspects, the unpleasant will seem minimal.

Imagine that a job assignment, or an event in your personal life, requires you to take a long airplane flight. The motivational surge you may get from participating in the activity might be neutralized if you think of the many negative aspects of travel: spending time in a crowded noisy airport; flight delays; a cramped and hot airplane; and passengers across the aisle sharing details of their life in loud voices. (You can tell how many natural rewards I find in airplane flights!)

Instead of thinking of the flight (assuming you dislike airports and airplanes) think of your destination, and why this trip is so important to you. Visualize being hugged by the person awaiting your arrival; and the trip's mechanics become of trivial significance.

To summarize this highly useful approach to developing self-leadership, use the following checklist. It will help you take advantage of the motivational power of natural rewards in your activities on the job and at home.

• Identify the pleasant, enjoyable aspects of your activities.

- Differentiate between (1) the rewarding aspects of the activities that are separate from the activity itself, and (2) the rewarding aspects that are built into the activity.
- Focus your thoughts on the pleasant rather than the unpleasant aspects of your work and personal activities.
- Focus more attention on the rewarding aspects of the activities that are part of the task itself rather than those that are separate from the task.

USING SELF-LEADERSHIP TO GET THROUGH UNINSPIRING TASKS

Practicing self-leadership is easier when you are performing a task you perceive as inherently enjoyable. A bigger challenge is to exercise self-leadership when you perceive the task at hand to be boring, routine, drudgery, or distasteful in any significant way. Under these circumstances, you have a self-motivation challenge. If you have already mastered the suggestions for overcoming procrastination, you have already developed some of the mental toughness you need to get through necessary but undesirable tasks.

Staying on track when the activity is unpleasant is the true test of self-discipline. I know a psychiatrist who persisted through medical school and the internship despite a strong dislike for most aspects of physical medicine. He enjoyed his residency because it involved psychiatry, not physical medicine. The psychiatrist analyzed his conundrum and solution in this way:

I remember wanting to be a psychiatrist since my high-school days. My parents wanted me to be a doctor so badly that they frequently bought me medical encyclopedias. When I was a little child I could count on medical kits for my birthday. My concerns about being a doctor were my hatred of the sight and touch of

87

blood, and my dislike of physically examining strangers. I chose psychiatry so I could be a "talking doctor"—one who cured people without touching them or seeing blood.

During college I found the zoology labs nauseating. At medical school and college I gritted my teeth when I had to see blood or touch patients. Yet, I did enjoy talking to patients, studying medical texts, and attending lectures. My attitude was that if I could only get through one more sight of blood, one more poking at a cadaver, I would be one step closer to becoming a psychiatrist. I was willing to put up with temporary misery to achieve my ultimate goal.

Four tactics are especially helpful in learning to exercise self-leadership to get you through tasks that are not inherently enjoyable.[8] These tactics follow closely some of the ideas in the self-discipline model on overcoming procrastination.

Set Goals for Yourself

As in all aspects of becoming more self-disciplined, goals play a central role. Consider Stephen, a victim of downsizing. Referred to an outplacement firm, the counselor advises him that the best way to find a new job is to make good use of his contacts. His specific assignment is to telephone 25 people in his network to request an informational interview.

Stephen hates rejection and dislikes deceiving people (he is looking for a job, not information) and so finds this task distasteful. He sets a realistic goal of five telephone calls a day for five days. Each call contains an element of pleasure because it brings him one step closer to achieving his daily goal. Each warm response will add a motivational surge.

Arrangement of Cues to Facilitate Your Behavior

On stage or off, a cue is a little signal that prompts you into action. With an undesirable task, prompts are particularly needed.

Making up to-do lists and posting reminders are a standard method of prompting you to complete a task that is not highly self-rewarding. Some people use the power-note system as a reminder. A power note is one posted in a highly visible place reminding you to do the day's most urgent activity, such as "calculate estimated tax payment," or "make appointment for replacing broken tooth."

The automobile service industry has been capitalizing on the motivational power of cues for about ten years. After an automobile is serviced, the technician places a transparent sticker on the upper left side of the windshield which lists the odometer reading (and sometimes date) when you are supposed to return for routine servicing again. Usually the sticker reminds you to return in 3,000 miles.

Self-Reward

When a task lacks many built-in motivators, I advise you to provide yourself with personally valued rewards for getting the onerous task completed. Stephen, who struggled through 25 job-search calls, might reward himself in this way: "After I complete these phone calls, I'm going to take an afternoon off from my job search to go swimming." Rewarding himself by taking an entire week off from his job search would have been escapist and self-defeating. The self-disciplined, self-leader chooses rewards wisely.

Self-Punishment and Self-Criticism

When you fail to perform an undesirable task, it is time to punish or criticize yourself sensibly. Recognize first that not accomplishing what needs to be done has built-in punishments. What if Stephen didn't make the phone calls demanded by the outplacement counselor? Two negative consequences are that he may not find a job quickly, and the outplacement counselor may give him short shrift.

Be creative in choosing a punishment that urges you to try harder but that simultaneously does not prompt you to become discouraged and task-avoidant. For some people a suitable punishment might be doing their most disliked household chore. (But even here, the self-disciplined person will find some pleasure within the task!)

If you choose self-criticism as a form of self-punishment, be sure not to engage in negative self-talk. Suppose you made a serious arithmetic error in a report you disliked preparing. A helpful self-criticism would be, "I'm angry with myself. I failed to double check my work, and it made me look foolish in my boss's eyes." A hurtful criticism would be, "I'm a complete fool. I always make mistakes in arithmetic because I'm stupid."

CHOOSING BETWEEN OPPORTUNITY AND OBSTACLE THINKING

Exercising self-leadership includes understanding the difference between looking at opportunities versus looking at obstacles. Manz believes that what we choose to think about is the most important part of self-leadership.[9] People who focus on opportunities will exercise more self-leadership than people who focus on obstacles. If you look mostly at opportunities, you will inspire yourself to high levels of performance and satisfaction. If you look mostly at obstacles, your life will move in the opposite direction. To understand the difference between opportunity and obstacle thinking, consider the following scenarios:

Scenario 1: Abundant Snow. Joan and Robert own and operate a convenience store. One night watching the weather report on television, they hear the forecaster warn of what could be the heaviest storm of the century coming into their area. As the couple looks out the window, the forecast is already coming true.

Robert, the obstacle-thinking partner, says, "This will kill our business for a few days. People will rush in to store up on supplies, then we'll hardly have any traffic. It could hurt our profits for the entire season."

In contrast, Joan, the opportunity-thinking partner, says, "What a great opportunity. We'll feature candles, flashlights, snow scrapers, soft drinks, beer, and snacks—all good sellers during a storm. Better yet, I'm getting up at three tomorrow morning. I'll drive our truck over to the snow-shovel distributor and buy every shovel they will sell me. We'll charge the full retail price, and sell out in no time. It may take me a while getting back if the storm is in progress, but it will be worth it. This is just the push we need to have a profitable winter season."

Scenario 2: Starting Over. Two friends, Gail and Debra, divorce their spouses at approximately the same time. Both women are in their mid-twenties and have two preschool children. Debra, the obstacle thinker, says, "This is the pits. I don't want to be alone in life. But I know it's going to be rough. Very few men want to date a woman with two young children."

Gail, the opportunity thinker, perceives the situation differently. She says to her friend: "One of the real concerns I had about Luke (her estranged spouse) is that he didn't appreciate family life. He wanted to be Prince Charming and a playboy. I think having two little children will be an asset in finding the type of man I want to meet. I'm going to place a personal ad, emphasizing that I'm looking for someone who enjoys family activities with young children."

You may recognize the concept of opportunity versus obstacle thinking as a variation of the half-full versus half-empty and optimism versus pessimism themes. Its familiarity, however, does not dismiss its relevance. Looking for the hidden opportunities in challenging situations is a success characteristic. Self-disciplined achievers inspire themselves to high performance and satisfaction by searching for possibilities. It takes more self-discipline to find opportunities because it's easy to think of the negatives. Yet if you can lead yourself to search for and find opportunities, you will have taken one more giant step toward becoming a self-disciplined achiever.

ACHIEVING QUALITY RESULTS

A continuing business thrust in companies of all kinds is to achieve high-quality goods and services. Programs and management systems too often are referred to as "total quality management" or "leadership through quality." Many quality initiatives have met with notable success, but others have failed completely. A leading cause of these failures is business's inability to see that quality programs are not the real reason companies improve their quality. Rather the true quality drivers are workers who are talented, dedicated, conscientious, and self-disciplined.

The purpose of this chapter is to show you how you can join the quality revolution by using self-discipline. You need to exercise self-discipline to achieve high quality, and, at the same time, a continuing quest for quality will improve your self-discipline. For example, if you clearly focus your mind on performing a task right the first time (a key principle of quality) you will improve your self-discipline.

MEASURING YOUR QUALITY ATTRIBUTES

To appreciate how your personal attributes play a major contribution to achieving quality, take the self-analysis on page 95. The quiz was developed by Craig Nathanson, a continuous improvement specialist at the Intel Corporation in Folsom, California.[1]

Achieving high quality on the job or at home requires a high degree of self-discipline. Without self-discipline as the fuel powering your quest for quality, your quality improvements may fizzle. The reciprocal relationship is also important: As you strive to become a quality person, you will also be strengthening your self-discipline.

One you complete the audit I'd like to direct your attention to the connection between self-discipline and the two major thrusts in the quality movement—total quality management and total customer satisfaction.

TOTAL QUALITY MANAGEMENT AND SELF-DISCIPLINE

Total quality management (TQM) is a management system for improving performance throughout an organization by maximizing customer satisfaction and making continuous improvements based on extensive employee involvement. Business firms,

(text continues on page 100)

ARE YOU A TOTAL QUALITY PERSON?

Circle the appropriate number for each item.

Personal leadership

Rarely Sometimes Always

1. I treat other people fairly and
   with respect.   1 2 3 4 5 6 7 8 9 10

2. I accurately listen to other
   people and don't interrupt to
   give my point of view.   1 2 3 4 5 6 7 8 9 10

3. I take responsibility for my
   actions and don't rely on others
   to plan my future.   1 2 3 4 5 6 7 8 9 10

4. I volunteer my services to help
   others in need.   1 2 3 4 5 6 7 8 9 10

5. I maintain a healthy, positive
   outlook on life.   1 2 3 4 5 6 7 8 9 10

6. I understand my values and
   apply them in my daily living. 1 2 3 4 5 6 7 8 9 10

7. My long- and short-term goals
   are tied to my values to ensure
   that what I'm doing in my life is
   important to me.   1 2 3 4 5 6 7 8 9 10

8. My daily activities are in
   harmony with my values.   1 2 3 4 5 6 7 8 9 10

9. I enjoy the people and things in
   my environment.   1 2 3 4 5 6 7 8 9 10

10. I practice good customer service
    with all the people with whom I
    come into contact.   1 2 3 4 5 6 7 8 9 10

self-analysis continues

Planning

11. Every day I take time to plan my daily activities around what is important to me.

1 2 3 4 5 6 7 8 9 10

12. I try to align my long- and short-term goals with my values to ensure that my daily activities are in harmony with my goals.

1 2 3 4 5 6 7 8 9 10

13. During my daily planning time, I prioritize both important and routine activities that I need to accomplish.

1 2 3 4 5 6 7 8 9 10

14. Each day I plan to accomplish only those activities for which I have allocated enough time.

1 2 3 4 5 6 7 8 9 10

15. I strive for continuous learning and have plans to further my education in areas that interest me.

1 2 3 4 5 6 7 8 9 10

16. I strive to work up to the standards set by the most accomplished people in areas that interest me.

1 2 3 4 5 6 7 8 9 10

17. I try to exceed the expectations of all those who come into contact with my activities.

1 2 3 4 5 6 7 8 9 10

18. When I plan my activities, I have knowledge of my environment and take any changing elements into consideration.

1 2 3 4 5 6 7 8 9 10

self-analysis continues

	Rarely Sometimes Always
19. I have a good sense of how my personal values, strengths, and weaknesses align with what I am doing.	1 2 3 4 5 6 7 8 9 10
20. I have thought out realistic goals with achievable targets for my major activities.	1 2 3 4 5 6 7 8 9 10

Improvement

Rarely Sometimes Always

21. I can document three major processes that I use in accomplishing my major goals.	1 2 3 4 5 6 7 8 9 10
22. I constantly strive to improve my skills, knowledge, and sense of purpose in my life's work.	1 2 3 4 5 6 7 8 9 10
23. I constantly strive to measure my success at meeting my personal goals.	1 2 3 4 5 6 7 8 9 10
24. I constantly strive to eliminate activities that have no value in my life and focus only on activities that enrich my life.	1 2 3 4 5 6 7 8 9 10
25. I admit my mistakes, acknowledge the reasons for them, and then move on with the intention of not making the same mistakes again.	1 2 3 4 5 6 7 8 9 10
26. I celebrate my successes and improvements.	1 2 3 4 5 6 7 8 9 10

self-analysis continues

97

Rarely Sometimes Always

27. I measure my successes by
    achieving my goals on time.   1 2 3 4 5 6 7 8 9 10

28. I constantly try to improve in all
    areas that are important to me and
    learn to accept my weaknesses in
    areas that don't interest me.   1 2 3 4 5 6 7 8 9 10

29. I am a role model for continuous
    improvement in everything I do.   1 2 3 4 5 6 7 8 9 10

30. I am open to changes in life that
    will enable me to learn new things. 1 2 3 4 5 6 7 8 9 10

Scoring and Interpretation

Add up the numbers you have circled and write the total: _____. The maximum score is 300 points. If you scored:

60–89 points:

Grade F. You might want to adopt some of these individual total quality strategies alluded to throughout the questionnaire to get your life back on track.

90–128 points:

Grade D. You might want to analyze your daily living patterns and goals in life. You do not demonstrate an individual total quality philosophy.

129–158 points:

Grade C. You demonstrate some patterns of a total quality person but need to be more consistent on a daily basis.

159–229 points:

Grade B. You have a good individual foundation in total quality principles and could serve as a role model for others.

230–300 points:

Grade A. You are a great total quality role model, with a solid set of principles in leadership, planning, and continuous improvement.

self-analysis continues

Let's see how a sampling of the statements in this audit relate to self-discipline.

Statement 3. I take responsibility for my actions and don't rely on others to plan my future. *Self-disciplined people are self-directing.*

Statement 5. I maintain a healthy, positive outlook on life. *Self-disciplined people frequently engage in positive self-talk.*

Statement 6. I understand my values and apply them in my daily living. *Self-disciplined people are powered by a mission statement reflecting their core values.*

Statement 7. My long- and short-term goals are tied to my values to ensure that what I'm doing in my life is important to me.

Statement 8. My daily activities are in harmony with my values.

Statement 12. I try to align my long- and short-term goals with my values to ensure that my daily activities are in harmony with my goals. *The preceding three items illustrate further that self-disciplined people are driven by a mission statement.*

Statement 13. During my daily planning time, I prioritize both important and routine activities that I need to accomplish.

Statement 14. Each day I plan to accomplish only those activities for which I have allocated enough time. *The preceding two items relate to the idea that self-disciplined people practice good time management and do not procrastinate.*

Statement 15. I strive for continuous learning and have plans to further my education in areas that interest me. *Self-disciplined people acquire the skills necessary to achieve goals.*

Statement 16. I strive to work up to the standards set by the most accomplished people in areas that interest me. *Self-disciplined people are influenced by appropriate role models.*

Statement 20. I have thought out realistic goals with achievable targets for my major activities. *Self-disciplined people set realistic goals.*

Statement 26. I celebrate my successes and improvements. *Self-disciplined people are proud of their accomplishments.*

Statement 27. I measure my successes by achieving my goals on time. *Self-disciplined people are goal-oriented.*

government agencies, health-care organizations, and educational institutions have joined the TQM bandwagon. Although programs labeled TQM may have lost some of their lustre, the push toward high quality remains. (Interestingly, one reason about one-third of TQM programs have flopped[2] is that they generated oppressive amounts of paperwork instead of concentrating on the transformational power of self-discipline.)

A major contributor to the success of quality-improvement programs is the personal characteristics of the workers providing the goods and services: intelligence, skill, and conscientiousness. Conscientiousness is, of course, a manifestation of self-discipline.

Let's see how self-discipline can have an impact on a sampling of total quality principles and techniques.

HAVE TEAM MEMBERS FIGURE OUT HOW TO ACHIEVE EXTRAORDINARY GOALS

A bold quality-enhancing leadership practice is to establish extraordinarily difficult quality targets for group members. In pursuing the extraordinary goal, team members are free to challenge any company rule or procedure that blocks attaining the goal. Coling Gilmore, an executive responsible for United Airlines's quality efforts in engine repair and maintenance, explains how the extraordinary-goal principle works:

> Tell people to increase quality by 5 or 10 percent and your message is basically, "Do what you've always done, but you'll just have to come to work earlier, skip lunch, and concentrate more." That's foolish and gets you nowhere. But if you tell people you want increases of 70 percent or so, first they'll scream bloody murder but then they'll realize this goal is to challenge every step and every person in the current process, and if necessary start from scratch.[3]

To achieve the extraordinary goal, the team members muster their self-discipline to concentrate on the problem facing them. Carefully focusing on the challenge, they ask questions such as:

- What steps are we taking that add no value to what we are producing?
- What assumptions are we making that are blocking good quality?
- Which people haven't we spoken to yet who might give us good clues to quality enhancement?

Quality expert Philip Crosby reasons that most human error is caused by lack of attention rather than lack of knowledge. And people are most likely to experience a lack of attention when they assume that error is inevitable.[4] For example, a bank teller might assume that being over or under $10 at the end of a busy day is good performance. But if he recognized his assumption about an inevitable error and pledged to make a conscious effort to do his job right the first time, he would make substantial progress in reducing quality errors.

People can approach "zero defects" only through a stringent application of self-discipline. The bank teller must stay focused all day on the mental image of not losing attention even for a moment. Balancing to the penny is the only acceptable performance from the standpoint of the zero-defects zealot.

Referring back to the self-discipline model, if the bank teller's mission statement includes becoming one of the leading performers in his bank, he is more likely to approach zero defects. Notice also that in accordance with the model, achieving high quality also includes goals (such as zero defects) and an action plan (all-day focus on mental image).

Another close-to-impossible goal is the 6-Sigma quality standard. It refers to work that is 99.9997 percent error free, or one defect in 3.4 million opportunities. The 6-Sigma standard has been achieved for several manufactured products, such as Kodak Gold film and the cans used to contain Pepsi soft drinks. Yet achieving the 6-Sigma standard is probably unreachable for products as complex as a luxury automobile or a consumer-products catalog.

Even with highly self-disciplined performers, there are certain human activities in which zero defects of the 6-Sigma standard have never been attained. Do you think a keyboarder/typist exists who has ever produced a 100-page document in which every stroke was right the first time? (A 6-Sigma standard for a typist would mean no errors in a 600-page manuscript.) Is there a basketball player who has played more than two games shot with 100 percent accuracy? Do you know of a sales representative who has attained a 100 percent closing average?

The purpose of improving your self-discipline is to substantially enhance your performance in key areas of work and personal life—*not to exceed human capability.* A combination of deliberate concentration and focusing on a goal will elevate your quality performance in most of life's activities.

THE PURPOSE OF IMPROVING YOUR SELF-DISCIPLINE IS TO SUBSTANTIALLY ENHANCE YOUR PERFORMANCE IN KEY AREAS OF WORK AND PERSONAL LIFE—NOT TO EXCEED HUMAN CAPABILITY.

Emphasize Continuous Improvement

Achieving total quality management is a gradual process, not a crash program. It fits well with the spirit of *kaizen*, a Japanese philosophy of continuing gradual improvement in one's personal and work life. Kaizen is a long-term gradual improvement process, involving a series of small, sometimes imperceptible changes. To follow kaizen is to be self-disciplined.

The spirit of kaizen heightens employee awareness to be constantly on the lookout for small improvements. Workers are also encouraged to look for things that are not quite right but are not yet full-blown problems. Paying attention to small details, such as checking to see if addresses on invoices are correct, fits the self-disciplined spirit of kaizen.

Avoid Complacency

To sustain high quality, meeting high standards is not enough. Unless you continue to strive for improvement (as in kaizen), you could become complacent and your standards of performance may lower gradually. To avoid complacency, most workers need frequent encouragement from the manager. Self-disciplined workers, in contrast, exercise self-leadership, and review their own performance in a detached, professional manner.

Consider Roberto, a repair technician. Using positive self-talk he encourages himself by asking, "How do today's activities contribute to my mission?" (Again, the mission statement you prepare in following the self-discipline model helps you achieve quality results.) Roberto wants to start his own heating and air conditioning sales and service firm. Every job he performs well now contributes to his mission by enhancing his reputation in the community.

TOTAL CUSTOMER SATISFACTION AND SELF-DISCIPLINE

Total quality aims at customer satisfaction, yet the idea of "total customer satisfaction" is even more explicit about satisfying and delighting customers. Self-discipline also plays a major role in satisfying customers. If you serve customers or clients directly, you need to work patiently and deliberately toward your goal of attaining and retaining their loyalty. You may also need the emotional self-control (a derivative of self-discipline) not to throttle your most demanding customers!

Let's examine a sampling of key principles of customer satisfaction, and see how self-discipline contributes to converting these principles into action. Knowledge of customer satisfaction principles coupled with the self-discipline to implement them *can* yield delighted, loyal customers.

Establish Customer-Service Goals

When embarking on improving customer service, you must decide how much help to give customers. Goal-setting of this type is a natural for the self-disciplined person because she integrates goal-setting into every phase of life. Answers are needed to such questions as:

- Is the company attempting to satisfy every customer within 10 minutes of his or her request?
- Is the company striving to provide the finest customer service in the field?
- Is the goal zero customer defections?

These goals will dictate how much, and the type of effort, you and other team members invest in pleasing customers. An awareness of levels of customer service (see the diagram on page 105) contributes to more precise customer-service goals. Goals at the highest level will move the company toward total customer satisfaction.

Assume that you were working toward the goal of providing the finest customer service in your field. With the help of your company, you would diligently search for information about the existing level of customer service provided by competitors. You would analyze what the competition is doing right and incorporate the best features into your plan for providing customer service. You would make lists reminding you to:

- Help resolve customer problems over the telephone after the sale

Levels of Customer Satisfaction

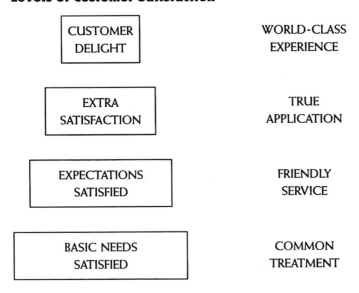

CUSTOMER DELIGHT	WORLD-CLASS EXPERIENCE
EXTRA SATISFACTION	TRUE APPLICATION
EXPECTATIONS SATISFIED	FRIENDLY SERVICE
BASIC NEEDS SATISFIED	COMMON TREATMENT

- Tell customers which competitor can help them if you do not have the product or service they need
- Give customers suggestions on how to make the best use of your product or service
- Explain patiently to customers when you think they might be misusing your product or service

As you deal with each customer you will diligently work from your action list and avoid getting sidetracked by distractions from other problems. Your unwavering goal is to make sure each customer walks away from you feeling she has received a good deal. You focus intently on customer needs just as a self-disciplined person is always focused on an important goal.

Create a Bond with Your Customer

A high-impact business concept is to bond, or form an emotional relationship, with customers. The rationale is that if you form warm, constructive relationships with your customers, they will keep buying. Such is the true meaning of relationship selling. Creating a bond is aimed at increasing sales, but it also enhances service. If the customer relies on and trusts the sales representatives, the customer will perceive the service to be of high quality. Similarly, people perceive medical and legal services to be of high quality if they trust the physician or lawyer.

Forming bonds with customers requires a high degree of self-discipline. You have to exert control over your behavior so you continually do things that are in the best interest of the customer. You have to avoid the distractions of avoiding short-term gain at the expense of a good long-term relationship. You have to keep the goal of relationship-building in mind during every interaction with a customer. Even the self-discipline of remembering to smile and say "See you again" can contribute substantially to forming a bond.

When you are attempting to capture the transformational power of self-discipline, visualize a bond with your customer. Create a sensory-rich mental image of your customer returning regularly for repeat business and calling you for your expert advice when problems arise. Picture your customer or client thanking you for good service.

Almost anything you do right with a customer will help form a bond. Here are eight techniques linked to self-discipline that are specifically aimed at bonding.

1. *Provide exceptional customer service.* Many successful companies contend their strategic advantage is good service. USAA, the fourth-largest insurer and financial services firm in the United States, has a much lower than industry average percentage of customer defectors. Its business grows primarily through referrals. USAA has no external salespeople and does not use insurance agents. Most customer concerns and inquiries are settled within minutes by calling

an 800 number. Robert F. McDermott, the recently retired CEO of USAA, said, "The mission and corporate culture of this company are, in one word, service."[5]

You don't have to be a large firm to create your own competitive advantage by developing a strategy of exceptional service. Incorporate a high level of service into your mission statement. As your actions mesh with your mission statement, you will be giving the type of service that creates bonds with customers.

2. *Understand the customer's business.* Successful people are emotionally involved with their work, so they are more likely to bond with a sales representative who understands their business or job. Time invested in understanding the customer's business often yields a large return. Establish the goal of learning about your customer's job or business to facilitate having the self-discipline to follow through.

> YOU DON'T HAVE TO BE A LARGE FIRM TO CREATE YOUR OWN COMPETITIVE ADVANTAGE BY DEVELOPING A STRATEGY OF EXCEPTIONAL SERVICE.

Sources of valuable information about customers include annual reports, newspaper and magazine articles, and trade magazines. Speaking to the customer's employees, suppliers, and customers will add to your knowledge base. Consistent with the self-discipline model, do not allow yourself to make excuses for not acquiring useful customer information.

3. *Show care and concern.* During contacts with your external or internal customer, show care and concern for the person's welfare. (An external customer is an outsider who pays for goods or service, whereas an internal customer is another worker who uses your output.) Ask questions such as, "How have you enjoyed the personal photocopier you bought a while back?" "How useful were the data I provided you?"

"How are you feeling today?" After asking the question, project a genuine interest in the answer.

If you are not the type of person who naturally projects care and concern, self-leadership will be needed to communicate concern. Make a mental note to yourself to ask the right questions and look sincere. The simple expedient of focusing your eyes on the customer's reactions will project sincerity.

4. *Make the buyer feel good.* A fundamental way of keeping a relationship going is to make the buyer feel good about himself. Also, customers should be made to feel good because they bought from you. An effective feel-good line is: "I enjoy doing business with you." Another one is: "You look bright and cheerful today." The self-disciplined person says to herself frequently, "My goal is to make my customer feel good. I'll do whatever it takes."

5. *Build personal relationships.* Building a good working relationship with a customer often leads to a positive personal relationship. A bolder approach is to do the reverse—build a working relationship based on a personal relationship. You gather personal facts about the interests of your customers and then appeal to those interests. To program your mind to use this tactic, imagine your customer or prospective customer as a friend. Think of what it would be like to shake the person's hand, or hug, upon meeting him for lunch. Jack, a bank president, gained considerable leverage by building personal relationships with customers.

Several years ago Jack was a commercial loan officer. He acquired a base of existing accounts from the previous officer and gradually increased it. Jack invested considerable time telephoning existing loan holders and, while in conversation, collected facts about them, such as birthdays, the names of family members, golf handicaps, hobbies, and favorite sport teams. Jack entered all this information into a computer.

On customers' birthdays and upon hearing about a special accomplishment, Jack would send greeting cards. When they came in for a meeting to talk about an existing loan or apply for a new one, Jack was able to incorporate his knowledge about them in conversation. His clients were so impressed that he received substantial referral business.

When Jack was hired by a competitor bank as the vice president of commercial loans, many of his old customers followed him when they sought new loans. Within several years Jack was promoted to bank president, becoming the youngest bank president in town. According to Jack, building personal relationships with customers is the single factor that distinguished him from other young bank officers. As president, he still keeps a file on major customers.

Jack used a number of tactics that are the signature of a self-disciplined person. Building a computer file on the personal preferences of his customers is a splendid act of self-discipline, as is retrieving facts about customers when they visited the bank.

6. *Make courtesy calls.* After a customer is in town, your relationship can be enhanced by an occasional courtesy call. The purpose of the telephone call, or personal visit, is to see how well the product or service is performing for your client. Making the courtesy call requires a heavy application of self-discipline because it may not have an immediate payback. Keep the reality principle in mind to program yourself to make courtesy calls. Be willing to postpone

short-term gratification for long-term gain. Courtesy calls are designed for long-term relationship-building. Nevertheless, many a quick sale has been made during one.

Ron, the owner and operator of an enormously busy and profitable business equipment distribution company, illustrates the effective application of courtesy calls. He attributes much of his store's success to a policy he has established for himself and his three sales representatives. Every customer receives a gentle follow-up call inquiring about how well the equipment is working and what unanswered questions remain. Ron and his sales representatives shy away from making a sales pitch during a courtesy call (restraint also requires self-discipline). However, if the customer inquires about a new machine or supplies, they respond affirmatively.

7. *Smile at every customer.* Smiling has many benefits—including lowering stress, decreasing wrinkles, and making a person more photogenic and telegenic. Smiling is also a natural relationship builder and can help you bond with your customer. (Customer training seminars often coach people on how to smile.)

Exercise the self-discipline to smile several times at each customer meeting, even if your customer is angry with your product or service. Smiling over the telephone is also important because it helps you achieve a warmer voice tone.

Not much self-discipline is required to smile when dealing with a warm, cheerful customer. Self-discipline is required, however, when you don't feel you have rapport with your customer and he is emotionally flat.

8. *Mirror your customer's behavior.* Rapport with a customer, or any other person, can often be improved through mirroring. To mirror someone is to subtly imitate that individual. It is one small aspect of *neurolinguistic programming,* a method of communication that combines features of hypnosis, linguistics, and nonverbal behavior. The components of this term help explain its relationship to self-discipline. "Neuro" refers to the way the human nervous system processes communication. "Linguistic" refers to the way that words, tone, timing, gestures, and inflection can be used in communication. "Programming" refers to using a systematic technique to communicate with others. When you use neurolinguistic programming you exercise control over your mind and behavior. To be successful at mirroring you have to concentrate intensely on the subtle movements of your target.

The most successful mirroring technique is to imitate another's breathing pattern. If you adjust your own breathing rate—through deliberate self-control—you will soon establish rapport. You might then imitate a few of your customer's most frequently used expressions. Be careful, however, not to blatantly ape your customer. Your potential bond could quickly break.

Several people I know who have experimented with mirroring think it has made some contribution to getting along better with an established customer. It is best to use mirroring as a supplement to the more orthodox techniques of forming bonds already described.

Focus on Solving Problems, Not Just Taking Orders

Self-discipline is virtually synonymous with staying focused. Knowing where to place your focus is critically important. To provide outstanding customer service, you must therefore place your focus on customer problems.

The focus on problem solving enables sales representatives to become partners in the success of their customers' businesses. By helping the customer solve problems, you can enhance the value of the supplier-customer relationship. Your customer will receive consulting services in addition to the merchandise or service being offered.

The self-discipline message here is that in most interactions with external or internal customers, you should ask yourself, "What problem can I help solve during our meeting?" Be alert to any signs of dissatisfaction or discontent the customer is experiencing. If a customer says, "We can barely keep up with our workload," it might be a cue for you to say, "We have a product that has helped many companies handle a larger workload." The problem-solving approach generally wins out over focusing on the merits of your product or service.

Solicit Customer Feedback Regularly

To stay attuned to customer needs, and therefore to provide quality service, solicit feedback from customers regularly. Many top-level managers follow this principle by regularly visiting company facilities that serve customers, such as stores, restaurants, and hotels. Bill Marriott of Marriott Corp. frequently visits the hotels in the company's chain. Customer feedback can also be obtained through surveys and careful study of telephone calls from customers.

Obtaining regular feedback requires self-discipline because it's easy to neglect seeking feedback in the everyday press of business activities. Yet feedback can provide clues to even higher levels of customer satisfaction—and therefore perceived quality.

Deal Constructively with Customer Complaints and Anger

Self-discipline in the form of emotional self-control is also important for achieving total customer satisfaction. In an era when customer satisfaction is so highly valued, both retail and industrial customers are likely to be vocal in their demands. When faced with an angry, picky customer the temptation might be to retaliate with a blast of vituperation. Instead, use one or more of the following techniques recommended by human relations specialist Donna Deeprose.[6]

1. *Acknowledge the customer's point of view.* Make statements such as "I understand," "I agree," and "I'm sorry" despite your urge to strike back. For example, if a customer says, "The accounts receivable department made a $1,000 overcharge on my account last month. If this doesn't get fixed right away I'm calling my lawyer." You might respond, "I understand how annoying this must be for you. I'll work on the problem right away."

2. *Avoid placing blame.* Suggesting that the customer is responsible for the problem intensifies the conflict. With the customer who claims to have been overcharged, exercise self-control not to question the customer's charge.

3. *Use six magic words to defuse anger.* The magic words are: I understand (that this is a problem); I agree (that it needs to be solved); I'm sorry (that this happened to you).

A key implication of these techniques for achieving quality results is that self-discipline makes a substantial contribution. As in most complex areas of life, having technical skill, talent, motivation, and knowing the facts are not enough to achieve extraordinary results. You also have to exercise self-discipline to consistently achieve total quality and total customer satisfaction.

CHAPTER 6

ENHANCING YOUR CREATIVITY

You might find it surprising that creative and imaginative thinking is another sphere of life in which self-discipline makes a major contribution—especially if you have attended creativity training and read books and articles about creativity, where nary a mention of self-discipline occurs. Of course, studying creativity and engaging in creativity-building exercises is only a beginning. Thinking and living creatively requires the discipline to actually integrate the principles and techniques of creativity into your everyday life.

To set the stage for using the power of self-discipline to enhance your creativity, let's first examine three misconceptions. Misconception one is that creative people are free spirits who lack self-discipline, and conversely that self-disciplined people are uptight, rigid, and unimaginative. In reality, creativity is usually the product of a self-disciplined mind. The creative thinker exercises self-discipline to search for one more alternative solution to the problem at hand.

Misconception two is that people can be conveniently classified as creative or noncreative. In truth, creativity can be looked at as a continuum, with some people populating the high end with great creative capabilities, some with limited resources populating the low end, and others in between with average capability. Because creativity is on a continuum, most people can improve their creative-thinking ability.

Misconception three is that creativity can only be exercised in a limited number of fields, such as physical science, the arts, advertising, and photography. An accurate analysis reveals that creativity can be exercised in any field and probably in any setting. You can exercise creativity in any job and in any facet of personal life.

DEVELOPING CREATIVE ATTITUDES AND THINKING PATTERNS

If you are guided by the reality principle (as described in Chapter 2) you are probably willing to invest the effort to bring about lasting improvements in your ability to think and act creatively. But first, why not take the creative Personality Test on page 116 and see where you are on the continuum.

Establish Creativity Goals

Surprise! A starting point in enhancing your creativity is to establish goals for becoming creative. As contained in the

(text continues on page 119)

CREATIVE PERSONALITY TEST

Answer each of the following questions as Mostly True or Mostly False.

	Mostly True	Mostly False
1. It is generally a waste of time to read articles and books outside my immediate field of interest.	_____	_____
2. I frequently have the urge to suggest ways of improving products and services I use.	_____	_____
3. Reading fiction and visiting art museums are time wasters.	_____	_____
4. What is right is right; what is wrong is wrong.	_____	_____
5. I enjoy it when my boss hands me vague instructions.	_____	_____
6. Making order out of chaos is actually fun.	_____	_____
7. Only under extraordinary circumstances would I deviate from my to-do list (or other ways in which I plan my day).	_____	_____
8. Taking a different route to work is fun, even if it takes longer.	_____	_____
9. Rules and regulations should not be taken too seriously. Most rules can be broken under unusual circumstances.	_____	_____

test continues

116

	Mostly True	Mostly False
10. Playing with a new idea is fun even if it doesn't benefit me in the end.	___	___
11. Some of my best ideas have come from building on the ideas of others.	___	___
12. When writing I try to avoid the use of unusual words and word combinations.	___	___
13. I frequently jot down improvements in the job I would like to make in the future.	___	___
14. I prefer to avoid using high-technology devices as much as possible.	___	___
15. I prefer writing personal notes or poems to loved ones rather than relying on greeting cards.	___	___
16. At one time or another in my life I have enjoyed doing puzzles.	___	___
17. If your thinking is clear, you will find the best solution to a problem.	___	___
18. It is best to interact with co-workers who think much like you.	___	___
19. Detective work would have some appeal to me.	___	___
20. Tight controls over people and money are necessary to run a successful organization.	___	___

test continues

117

Scoring and Interpretation

Give yourself one point for each correct answer as indicated below:

1. Mostly False	8. Mostly True	15. Mostly True
2. Mostly True	9. Mostly True	16. Mostly True
3. Mostly False	10. Mostly True	17. Mostly False
4. Mostly False	11. Mostly True	18. Mostly False
5. Mostly True	12. Mostly False	19. Mostly True
6. Mostly True	13. Mostly True	20. Mostly False
7. Mostly False	14. Mostly False	

Total _____

Extremely high or low scores are the most meaningful. A score of 15 or more suggests that your personality and attitudes are similar to those of creative people. A score of 8 or less suggests that you are more of an intellectual conformist at present. Don't be discouraged. Most people can develop in the direction of becoming more creative. If you acquire knowledge of general principles and specific techniques of creativity improvement and apply them in a self-disciplined way, you can enhance your creativity.

How does your score compare to your self-evaluation of your creativity? I suggest you also obtain feedback on your creativity from somebody familiar with your thinking and your work. Compare his or her evaluation of your creativity with your test score.

self-discipline model, goals are a key component of being self-disciplined. Creativity goals should specify why you are engaging in creative thinking. You are much more likely to discipline yourself to think creatively when you are committed to achieving a specific outcome. Here is a sampling of creativity goals:

- By May 31, I will arrive at a new idea for a family vacation.
- By January 15, I will uncover five new methods of meeting men that I have not tried before.
- By 6:00 p.m. tonight I will think of a way to trim $100,000 from our department budget without damaging productivity or morale.
- By Sunday at 4:00 p.m. I will think of a radically different setting for a family photo portrait.

With goals clearly in mind, you can focus your energy on finding a creative alternative. I first tried this technique after giving an after-dinner talk in Erie, Pennsylvania. My return trip home was a three-and-one-half-hour ride on the New York State Thruway. To enhance the productivity of my trip beyond listening to news and music on the radio, I decided to set a creativity goal. By the time I arrived home, I would be committed to the best research idea I thought of during my trip back. I equipped myself with a felt-tip pen and yellow pad so I could jot down ideas in large handwriting to be deciphered the next day. As I drove along I forced myself to write down any topic I could think of, however feeble. Every 15 minutes or so I had at least something to jot down.

Two miles away from my highway exit, a useful idea finally surfaced—conducting research on overcoming adversity. For fifteen years now I have been conducting research and writing about that topic. How's that for a productive car trip? Next time you're on a long journey, set a creativity goal for yourself. Your idea could pay enormous career dividends.

Visualize Your Way to Enhanced Creativity

The importance of imagery in creativity is underscored by the word *image* as the root of imagination. Most discoveries and useful ideas begin with a flash of imagination. The image is usually visual but can also be auditory, olfactory (smell), or gustatory (taste). If you have been using the self-discipline model, you have already worked hard to improve your visualization. The specific conditions under which these images most often occur to creative people are varied: riding in a vehicle, walking, listening to music, reading, watching television, bathing or showering, and concentrating on an object.

Working at a computer often facilitates the concentration needed to trigger visualization. Altered states of consciousness attributed to alcohol and other drugs are also known to produce useful images for creativity.[1]

The fact that creative ideas often stem from concentrating on an object helps explain the contribution of self-discipline to creativity. If you stay focused on the task at hand, a creative idea is likely to surface. (The idea-search while driving is another application of this principle.) Have you ever stared at a problem for about 5 minutes, to find that an imaginative solution suddenly came to mind? If you did, you have already used self-discipline to help you visualize a solution to a problem.

The most important suggestion here is for you to discipline yourself to concentrate. Then just let it happen. With frequent practice, useful ideas will just seem to bubble up.

Overcome Traditional Mental Sets

A unifying theme runs through all forms of creativity training and suggestions for creativity improvement: creative problem solving

ENHANCING YOUR CREATIVITY

requires an ability to overcome *traditional thinking*. The concept of traditional thinking is relative but generally refers to a standard and frequent way of finding a solution to a problem. A traditional solution to a problem is thus a modal or recurring solution. Raising money by conducting a garage sale is an example of a traditional solution to a problem.

The creative person looks at problems in a new light and transcends conventional thinking about them. For many years, banks were unable to solve the problem of how to decrease the cost of customer withdrawals. (They succeeded in decreasing the cost of customer deposits by developing night deposit devices which let customers deposit cash into a mailbox-style drop using a key.) John Diebold, the automation pioneer, finally posed the right question: "Why not find a way to allow customers to deposit and withdraw money automatically?" This seminal thought led to the automatic teller machine (ATM).

WORKING AT A COMPUTER OFTEN FACILITATES THE CONCENTRATION NEEDED TO TRIGGER VISUALIZATION.

The central task in becoming creative is to break down rigid thinking that blocks new ideas.[2] Self-discipline can help you increase mental flexibility so that faced with a problem, you keep digging for one more—the best—solution. (By postponing the immediate gratification of taking the first solution that comes along and waiting for a better one, you are being guided by the reality principle.)

> Several years ago, a college student was running short of ideas for raising money to meet education expenses. After trying most of the standard ideas, he placed a classified ad in a local newspaper inviting people to invest in his future. Several executives were so impressed with his creativity and chutzpa that they lent him a total of $40,000 in education loans and outright gifts.

Overcoming traditional mental sets can be approached from several perspectives. Here are eight:

1. *Learn to think outside the "box."*

A box in this sense is a category that confines and restricts thinking. To think outside the box, you have to confront your *functional fixedness*—the inability to consider more than one (or a fixed) function for an object. For instance, only playing baseball with a baseball bat.

2. *Avoid hardening of the categories.*

A noncreative person thinks categorically, such as "Only men can climb telephone poles," or "Only women can work in child care centers as caregivers." Make your categories permeable by thinking more inclusively. If you want to begin a program of physical exercise, avoid the trap of saying to yourself, "When you need to exercise, join a health club." Instead, ask yourself, "What alternatives are there for joining a health club?" You will find a variety of ways to achieve your physical fitness goals, including taking

---

THINKING OUTSIDE THE BOX

Visualize a table with three objects on top: a candle, a box containing six thumbtacks, and a book of matches. Your problem is to explain how a candle can be mounted on the wall in back of the table. (The solution to the problem appears at the end of this chapter.) If you can think of a way to mount the candle on the wall you are skillful at overcoming functional fixedness. If you are stuck, keep concentrating and attempt to visualize an answer. For additional practice in overcoming functional fixedness, think of ten uses for a safety pin, a razor blade, a brick, and a wine bottle.

---

on heavy projects around the house. Of course, you will have to exercise self-discipline to participate in physical exercise on your own.

3. *Challenge your assumptions.*

A powerful method of overcoming traditional mental sets is to question the assumptions you make as you attempt to solve problems. Challenging your assumptions is difficult because many assumptions are so ingrained that people do not even realize they are assumptions.

Suppose you decide that you want a new dining room set because your present one is falling apart, unesthetic, and it disturbs you every time you see it. Your decision to obtain a new dining room set is therefore rational. However, you wonder if you can afford one considering the many unanticipated expenses facing you. Stop right now! You are assuming you have to *purchase* a new dining room set. Challenging the assumption that new dining room sets have to be purchased leads you to alternatives. What can you offer to barter for another set? Being strong and nimble, you place a classified ad expressing your willingness to paint somebody's house in exchange for an acceptable dining room set. Or you might exchange your second computer, or a set of collectibles. Maybe a furniture store owner will call you and barter a new set, or maybe you will find a used set.

4. *Create and use an idea file.*

Good ideas are hard to come by, yet they are readily forgotten in the press of normal activities. A standard creativity improvement device of people who are dependent upon novel ideas for their livelihood is to keep an idea file with them at all times—including one at bedside. The idea file is most often a notebook but can also be a laptop computer or a file box. Keeping a supply of Rollodex cards in your wallet is effective because you can file them upon returning home.

When an idea of any possible merit flashes across your mind, exercise the self-discipline to enter it in your file reserved for that purpose. But don't think of this as a *storage* file, which is seldom opened. Your idea file is living and should be referred to frequently to see which ideas are ready for refinement and implementation.

5. *Become immersed in your work.*

More than a vivid imagination is required to be creative. A wealth of knowledge in the area in which you are working is also needed to process and combine information. If you have incorporated the self-discipline component, "search for pleasure within the task," you have already made strides toward work immersion. The importance of having facts and details at your disposal increases when you consider that creativity is the association of previously uncombined tasks.

The person who thought of an electronic city hall, for example, had to be aware of such facts as (a) the demands made on local governments, (b) the services offered by local governments, (c) computer capabilities, and (d) automatic teller machines.

Becoming immersed in your work requires a dose of self-discipline: Ensure you spend an average of 15 minutes a day gathering information of potential value. Search for ideas in print, on television and radio, and from listening directly to knowledgeable people. Some of your best information may arise when browsing your way through a publication you ordinarily do not have time to read thoroughly.

6. *Maintain an enthusiastic attitude.*

A major hurdle in becoming a creative problem solver is resolving the conflict between being judicial and imaginative. In many work and personal situations, being judicial (or judgmental) is necessary. Situations calling for judicial thinking include reviewing proposed expenditures, inspecting products for quality or safety defects, and evaluating how much one can afford to spend on a wedding. Imaginative thinking is necessary when searching for creative alternatives. Alex F. Osburn, a former advertising executive and the originator of brainstorming, notes how judgment and imagination are often in conflict:

> The fact that moods won't mix largely explains why the judicial and the creative tend to clash. The right mood for judicial thinking is largely negative. "What's wrong with this? . . . No, this won't work." Such reflexes are right and proper when trying to judge. In contrast, our creative thinking calls for a positive attitude. We have to be hopeful. We need enthusiasm. We have to encourage ourselves to the point of self-confidence. We have to beware of perfectionism lest it be abortive.[3]

The action step is therefore to project yourself into a positive frame of mind when attempting to be creative. The same principle applies when attempting to be creative about a judicial task. For instance, you might be faced with the task of looking for creative ways to cut costs. You would then have to think positively about thinking negatively!

You can project enthusiasm by remembering to look for the pleasure within the task and using positive self-talk. Say to yourself, "I'm going to look for the positive elements in this situation and comment on them." A self-disciplined mind is programmed to meet the requirements of the moment.

7. *Identify your creative time period.*

As you discipline yourself to make creativity a habit, it helps to identify those times of the day or week when your capacity for creative thought is the highest and the lowest. For most people, creative capacity is high following ample rest, so it's best to tackle problems requiring creative solutions at the start of a day. Some executives and researchers tackle their biggest thought problems while on vacation or exercising. The solution to the problem is conceptualized, and the details are worked out on the job.

> FOR MOST PEOPLE, CREATIVE CAPACITY IS BEST FOLLOWING AMPLE REST, SO IT IS BEST TO TACKLE PROBLEMS REQUIRING CREATIVE SOLUTIONS AT THE START OF A DAY.

Other individuals report that their best time for creative thought is immediately before falling asleep. For them, the idea file adjacent to the bed is indispensable for jotting down nocturnal flashes of inspiration. (Record your idea, and then pay attention to your partner.) One manager reports that she gets her best ideas during meetings conducted for other purposes. The point is to chart your individual creative time periods.

8. *Develop a synergy between both sides of the brain.*

It is generally believed that the left side of the brain is the source of most analytical, and logical, thought. It performs the tasks necessary for well-reasoned arguments and working with standard applications of a computer. The right side of the brain grasps the work in a more intuitive, overall manner. It is the source of impressionistic, creative thought.

People with dominant right brains thrive on disorder and ambiguity—both characteristics of creative people.

Current scientific thought indicates that any mental activity is carried out by both sides of the brain simultaneously. Joined by a connecting link called the corpus callosum, the two hemispheres work together in harmony. Creative thought arises from the symbiotic cooperation of various parts of the brain in both the left and right hemispheres. Therefore the highly creative individual achieves synergy (the combination is more than the sum of the parts) between the two sides of the brain. Both brain hemispheres are used as needed.

Self-discipline is needed to move you toward developing the brain synergy so characteristic of creative people. Focus carefully at times on being the logical fact-gatherer and processor. Be judicial and stern. Solve problems in a step-by-step analytical way. At other times, focus on being intellectual and playful. Visualize freely, and let your imagination run wild. Think of yourself shifting back and forth between the roles of advertising copywriter and advertising executive.

SPECIFIC CREATIVITY-ENHANCING TECHNIQUES

The attitudes and thinking patterns just described prepare you for becoming more creative. If applied diligently, you will gradually become more creative. You can also incorporate specific creativity techniques into your daily activities. You've probably engaged in brainstorming or are generally familiar with the technique. Here I direct your attention to less widely known techniques. But remember you need a disciplined, focused approach to reap big rewards from whichever technique you choose to apply to a real problem.

Conduct Solo Brainstorming Sessions

Brainstorming is widely recognized as a group method of finding creative alternatives to problems. A variation that you can use working alone is *solo brainstorming*. The technique is sometimes called *brainwriting* because you write down the ideas that come into your brain. To use this technique, you record a number of alternative solutions to a problem; it often helps to give yourself a quota of ideas along with a deadline.

Much self-discipline is required to conduct brainwriting because you don't have the support of the group. Faced with a situation calling for a creative response, you might sit quietly with a pencil and paper, computer, or tape recorder and begin to generate solutions. For example, "How can I shorten the time it takes our customers to pay their bills without creating ill will?" Most people accept the first one or two alternatives to such a problem. Through solo brainstorming, you can learn to search for many alternatives.

Solo brainstorming is the essence of creative thinking and problem solving. Some creative problem solvers experience a burst of inspiration when they first tackle a problem. Most others patiently sift through alternatives until the right one surfaces. Thomas Edison and his team, for example, tested 60,000 substances on the path to the successful invention of the alkaline battery.

Edison's persistence has a message. Discipline yourself to explore at least six plausible alternatives for each significant work or personal problem. (I realize you don't have the time to pursue 60,000 alternatives to your problem.) Most people are pleasantly surprised to find that so many ideas are lurking in the recesses of the brain, just requiring the right dose of self-discipline to be released.

The Random-Word Technique

If you are ready to stretch your imagination, I recommend the random-word technique, both as a method of developing flexible thinking and solving real problems. The random-word technique is based on the assumption that making remote associations is an important part of the creative process. The technique forces people to make a useful association to a concrete word chosen at random, usually from a dictionary or thesaurus. Here is how the approach worked effectively for a well-known company, according to creativity consultant Bryan W. Mattimore:

> A highly successful line of Campbell's soups was born in a random-word brainstorming session. The dictionary word was "handle." This led them to "utensil," and finally "fork." "The soup you can eat with a fork!" someone joked. You can't eat soup with a fork. But the unconscious mind, seizing the idea hook, supplies another answer instantly: ". . . unless it's incredibly full of meat and vegetables and other good stuff." Thus, Campbell's "Chunky" soups.[4]

To use the random-word technique successfully, two guidelines are especially important. Notice the mention of "concrete word." My experience in conducting this technique is that the stimulus word you choose influences the effectiveness of the technique. Nouns and adjectives (such as "iron" or "light") work best. You therefore are allowed to reject random words that are not nouns or adjectives (for instance, a pronoun) and you can reject one noun or adjective—but only once. If you have too many preemptory challenges, you will look for words that fit preconceived solutions to your problem.

The second guideline relates directly to a component of the self-discipline model: minimize excuse making. Assume you have rejected a pronoun and exercised your right to reject one concrete word and have now selected your stimulus word—even if it's "no better" than your first choice. You must now force yourself to make associations to the stimulus word. Make no excuses about the stimulus word leaving you flat or being unsuited to your problem. Keep trying until some meaningful association surfaces. All creative problem-solving methods ultimately force the problem solver to exercise the discipline to keep scratching for alternative solutions.

The random-word technique can be as useful at home as it is at work. A single mother, Jan, employed by a commercial printing company had a nine-year-old daughter. She planned to begin an investment program to help pay college expenses for her daughter with the salary increase she was expecting the following year. An unanticipated development occurred; her employer froze wage increases for a year as a money-saving measure.

Exasperated, Jan began thinking of other ways to raise the money using the random-word technique—which she learned about in a company seminar. The first random word her finger landed on was "Barcelona." Reject. Next her finger hit upon "zebra." Must do. Jan was skeptical but had the self-discipline to forge ahead. Her mental process proceeded as follows:

A zebra is a big animal found in zoos and in Africa. Maybe I should sell zebra figurines on the street corner. No good. Street vendors make almost nothing. Not enough zebra lovers here in Philadelphia. Wait a minute, maybe I could sell zebra-striped T-shirts. I could appeal to people who are proud of their African heritage. That won't work. Most African-Americans probably don't associate zebras with the homeland of their ancestors. Worse, I'm Asian. I wouldn't appear authentic selling a product with an African appeal.

A zebra is black and white, I could become a photographer specializing in black-and-white photographs. That's crazy. I'm strictly an aim and shoot rank amateur. Also, there's not much of a market for black-and-white photographs except for newspapers and X-rays. Wow, I'm on to something. Amateur and zebra go together. Basketball referees are sometimes called zebras because their shirts are striped black and white. There's always a need for more referees for amateur basketball teams. I've refereed a little in the past. I'll polish my skills and then seek work as a basketball referee. I'll invest every penny I make, and Jody can come to the games unless she's with her father.

Jan now referees several games a month, investing her earnings into the college fund. After her company's wage freeze was over she received a salary increase. She disciplined herself to invest the increase along with the "zebra earnings." Jody's education fund is growing rapidly.

The Excursion Method

This is based on making word associations related to the problem. The association can be to another word or object:

The leader of a company safety and health group wanted to increase the visibility of the group. During a problem-solving meeting, team members were asked to take an excursion with (or free associate to) the word visibility. Among the word associations made were: big, tall, bright-colored, shining light, no fog, sunny day, media coverage, and television. An indirect but powerful link between the word television and the problem flashed in the group leader's mind. The word television related to video. What about becoming more visible by making a videotape showcasing the group? Copies of the videotape could then be sent to executives around the company who could watch it at their leisure. Perhaps they could also encourage their staff members to watch the video.

The group ultimately prepared a videotape that explained the safety and health group's mission and some of its accomplishments. The video, in turn, led to more exposure, including coverage in the company newsletter.

Self-discipline is necessary when using the excursion method because you have to concentrate and stay focused. Your mind should wander—but *within* the framework of the task, not outside it.

You Are the Product

Are you ready for some heavy-duty visualization? A role-playing exercise well-suited to new product development and creativity enhancement is called "You are the product." The core of the technique is for participants to pretend that they are a product and discuss how being that product makes them act, feel, or perceive.[5]

Creativity consultant Jim Ferry had executives at Pitney Bowes invent new product ideas for a postage meter. The team accomplished this by forming a human postage meter, with each executive playing a different part of the machine. One "part" of the machine said, "I'm just glad I wasn't the envelope sealer." His visualization related to the hard work performed by this part of the machine, suggesting the need for an extra-strength part (or maybe he was concerned about being an official licker).

At Rich Products Company, the task was to name a new healthy dessert topping for sale to restaurant owners. One person played the role of the dessert, one played the topping, and another the dessert eater. The dessert said he "didn't want something too heavy to lift." The topping said she wanted to befriend the dessert so she could "get along with him well." The dessert eater explained, "I don't want anything too messy." Top Life was the winning name, particularly because it implied a dessert topping for a healthy lifestyle. Notice the playful imagination required to develop ideas for this role play.

Ferry also held a successful new product development session at the Polymer Technologies Division of Bausch & Lomb. Executives were paired off in teams, with one playing the eyeball and another Bausch & Lomb's rigid gas-permeable contact lens. The eyeball-person persistently requested a pillow to cushion the hard and "insensitive" contact lens. The result was a new research initiative by the Polymer Division to bond a special space-age cushioning material directly onto the contact lens. The more eye-friendly contact lens has been a commercial success.

Applying "you are the product" to areas outside new product development requires imagination. Suppose your unit of the company issues contracts. Imagine you are the contract that is supposed to be issued to a customer. Think of how you would feel being routed from one department to another, waiting for approvals from seven different people. Imagine how lonely it would be waiting in the corporate attorney's in-box for five days. Your goal is to be sent to your true home, the customer's office. Think of how you would fight and squirm to avoid having so many people decide on your fate.

"You are the product" also has potential application for improving your personal life. Suppose you wanted to design a family room so it best meets the needs of family members. Visualize yourself as a family room attempting to take care of everybody. You might say, "I want to be a comfortable haven for everybody, but I dislike being trashed. I hate it when people tromp on my carpet with shoes they've worn outside. I hate the mud, the oil stains, and the street filth. Maybe I'll locate on the side of the house and keep a boot tray outside. I want to be modern, so I'll offer my constituents wrap-around sound, video games, and a powerful computer with a modem for contact with the outside world."

Use Creative Dreaming

Dreaming is an eminently creative process. People who do not perceive themselves as creative fabricate elaborate plots while dreaming. Dreamers often project themselves into places they have never been, dealing with people they have never seen. Furthermore, they carry out activities they have never done previously. Self-discipline is not involved in spontaneous dreaming because it occurs without conscious effort. When your brain is in an altered state of consciousness, such as with a fever, your dreams are likely to be wilder (more imaginative) than ever. Adding to the mystery of dreams, some people experience a similar dream whenever they have a fever.

Self-discipline can help you capitalize on the creative powers of dreams, even though the process is slow and indirect. Business creativity expert Bryan W. Mattimore has found a way people can capture the creative power of dreams. The method is to regularly feed the mind with problems to solve.[6] Before going to sleep give your mind a problem to solve, such as how to meet a person who will eventually become your spouse. You thus use dreams to meet the person of your dreams. Feeding your subconscious mind a problem to solve may not work upon first application. You have to train it by repeating the process many times and exercise self-discipline to concentrate on feeding your mind the problem. Soon your subconscious mind will respond to your requests. Eventually your dreams will contain solutions to the problems you face.

EVENTUALLY YOUR DREAMS WILL CONTAIN SOLUTIONS TO THE PROBLEMS YOU FACE.

Encouraging your subconscious mind to work on problems while you are dreaming is one major step in using creative dreaming. The other is to learn to interpret your dreams, because dreams often come in symbols and metaphors. Reflect back now to the make-believe example of requesting your subconscious to help you find Mr. or Ms. Right. A few nights after making this request, you dream of going to the zoo with your oldest cousin, Chris. Upon awaking you say to yourself, "A dream of a pleasant childhood memory, but it certainly doesn't help me find a mate."

I challenge you to dig deeper for symbols. Chris is the first name of your oldest cousin, but isn't there a Chris in your office whom you find quite attractive? Maybe Chris would like to get a relationship going with you. Overcome your shyness, and ask Chris to join you for lunch or an after-hours beverage. Your dream has given you a signal that the person of your dreams is somebody you already know, and whose name evokes pleasant memories.

Using the creative power of dreams to solve problems is more speculative than any other method presented in this chapter. You are more likely, for example, to get a quick return on self-disciplined effort when using solo brainstorming or the random-word technique. Yet dreams may yield a more imaginative, more complex solution to a problem. A screenwriter can use dreams to find a story line. An advertising copywriter can use dreams to identify the theme to an advertising campaign. And anybody can use dreams to find a mission in life. If you still have yet to formulate your mission statement, discipline your subconscious to get working on the project.

The Napoleon Technique

Another creativity-enhancing technique for people who enjoy visualization is to assume another identity. The Napoleon Technique is particularly applicable when you face a repeated, intractable dilemma. The new identity you assume helps you look at the problem from a different perspective.

Creativity consultant Roger von Oech was asked to help generate ideas for icons (tiny images that represent different functions) for the Macintosh computer. Von Oech fantasized into the exercise a number of famous participants. Of those fantasized participants, game show celebrity Vanna White contributed the most useful idea.

White's imagined presence made the problem-solving group think of turning letters, then of attractive women. Finally, the term *airhead* also surfaced. Flash. The new icon chosen was a vacuum cleaner to represent a function that collects things from one place on the screen and deposits them elsewhere.[7] (Note carefully that free association took place. No group member accused White, or attractive women in general, of being an airhead. The association just meant that at least one group member recalled an attractive woman who he or she perceived as being an airhead.)

To apply the Napoleon Technique to a problem facing you, project somebody you admire into the scene. Perhaps you can take one of the role models you are using in your development of self-discipline.

Jim, the owner of a large automobile service station, was facing lower-than-anticipated business volume. One key problem was that a Goodyear service center recently opened, thus increasing the competition. Jim was an admirer of General Colin Powell, so he assumed the identity of Powell who had arrived in town to help the service station improve business. Jim began to free associate: "Powell would make people salute; he wouldn't put up with any nonsense; technicians would wear uniforms; the place would be as clean as command headquarters." Big flash of business insight. The dealer decided to have his technicians wear uniforms and keep his place as clean as the Goodyear dealership. Business did improve gradually.

Create a Collage

Sometime in your life you have probably cut and pasted magazine photos and drawings to form a collage. Maybe your third-grade teacher had you assemble a collage of "My favorite farm animals." Maybe as a teenager you fabricated a collage of the sexiest men or sexiest women. Maybe you created a collage of the "world's most beautiful cars."

Collages can also be used to help you prepare important visuals, such as an ideal product for your company, the development of a sales presentation, or ideas for a dramatic speech.[8] Related to the components of self-discipline, you can use this creative technique to update and refine your mission statement. Cut and paste photos of people you admire carrying out activities you admire. Include people at work and at play.

The process of creating your collage will enhance your ability to visualize, thus strengthening your self-discipline. Collage making is so inherently enjoyable and requires less self-discipline to implement than most other creativity techniques.

Be Alert to Opportunities

I conclude with a creativity-enhancing technique that could also be regarded as an attitude or thinking pattern. To function as a creative person, you need to discipline yourself to spot opportunities that other people overlook. As facts present themselves, ask yourself questions such as:

"Is there an opportunity hidden in this situation?"

"What significance should I attach to the data I have just observed?"

"If I were forced to make a living out of the opportunities in the facts I just observed, what would I do?"

Fred Sarkis, a man with considerable entrepreneurial experience, noticed that many health-conscious people are concerned about their blood pressure. He also observed that vending machines to measure blood pressure were in limited supply. His alertness to this opportunity triggered a successful idea for a family business. Two family members install and operate coin-operated blood-pressure machines. Fred says that he and his son are making money, having fun, and performing a social good.

In family and personal life also, having the self-discipline to spot opportunities can enhance your life. As you read newspapers, magazines, books, watch television, listen to the radio, and observe people in action be alert to information that can enhance your life. For example, you might read about a program whereby impoverished children from an underdeveloped country are spending summers with host families in your country. You might say, "Hey, let's give it a try."

Bringing happiness to an unfortunate child and to your family is but one of the hundreds of possible benefits stemming from the transformational power of self-discipline. In this application of self-discipline keep in back of your mind that you are a proactive opportunity seeker.

Solution to Thinking Outside the Box

Affix the small box to the wall with the thumbtacks. Then place the candle on top of the box. Strengthen the attachment by dripping some wax from the candle, lighting it with the matches. The bond can be strengthened by inserting a thumbtack from underneath, going through the underside of the top of the box.

CHAPTER 7

SUCCEEDING
AT PERSONAL
DEVELOPMENT

With a freshly minted MBA, Cheryl aspired to a career in international banking. She landed a job as an assistant to the president at a bank in Gary, Indiana—a fine job but a far cry from international banking. Cheryl told her friends and several of her professors, "I'm taking this job now, but it's only until I build up my credentials for international banking and finance. All I have to do is to take a few courses on international currency. I've had some experience with it, but I need to come up to speed."

And so, Cheryl enrolled in a course. In addition to attending class, she devoted about one hour a week to studying. Unfortunately, as her work responsibilities increased, Cheryl found the course an interference. Two weeks before the course would have ended, Cheryl dropped out. She rationalized, "At least I've made a start. Next year, I'll really apply myself." *Adios* Cheryl, *mañana* is not time enough for your career.

Perhaps I should be more tolerant of Cheryl. She is not alone. Self-improvement in any significant way is a tough challenge. Most people who embark upon a program of self-improvement or personal development start with a burst of enthusiasm. Being well-motivated initially, they quickly acquire knowledge and skill. Within several months, however, something goes wrong.

Many people who try to enrich their lives significantly find that progress hits a wall early. Somehow they lose interest in what they are trying to accomplish. Or they complain that they can no longer spare the time. Others who do make legitimate gains in improving themselves find that they have forgotten the new knowledge and skills they invested so much time in acquiring. Even more disappointed are those people who cannot keep up the pace of self-improvement. Somehow they don't follow through enough to sustain initial gains.

The key barrier to self-improvement and personal development faced by so many aspirants is the inability to marshall enough self-discipline. With the proper application of self-discipline, many forms of self-improvement are possible. My purpose in this chapter is to show you how your self-improvement efforts will be more successful if you have a keen understanding of how you can change your own behavior and attitudes and retain information.

A LEARNING SYSTEM FOR SELF-IMPROVEMENT

Changing behavior requires you to learn new behavior. And, like any learning effort, following a basic system will enhance your success. I'd like to present to you a four-part learning system for self-improvement. To change your behavior, you need a goal, and a way to measure your current reality against this goal. You also need a way to react to affect the reality with an action plan and a way to obtain feedback on the impact of your new actions.[1]

Goal or Desired State of Affairs

Changing your behavior requires a clear goal or a vision of a desired state of affairs. Only with a goal will you have sufficient motivation to exercise the necessary self-discipline for success. Self-improvement goals can be varied or quite specific; for example, learning how to line-dance, speak a new language fluently, or operate an advanced camera. Consider Fred, a young business professional who wants to develop his political skills to advance his career. His goal is to acquire power, and developing political skill is really an action plan to acquire such power.

Assessing Reality

The second major requirement for a learning system, or method of changing behavior, is to assess reality. Fred needs a way to assess how much power he currently possesses and to measure his level of political skill, since he is convinced that improved political skill will enhance his promotability. Assessing reality can be straight-forward and concrete—or complex and abstract.

Fred knows his present position in his company's hierarchy. As a marketing manager, on the organization chart he is five levels below the executive suite (even though the firm had eliminated two layers of management). To assess his potential for career growth in the firm, Fred needs to take a few actions: (1) pay careful attention during his next performance appraisal to what his manager says about his promotability; (2) review his previous performance appraisals for comments that may have been made about his promotability; (3) assess development and progress by asking himself questions such as:

- Has the company been sending me to management development or leadership development seminars?
- Am I ever introduced to important people in the company?
- Have I been assigned to any important task forces or committees?
- Do I receive only routine e-mail?
- Does anybody above my level ask my opinion on important topics relating to the welfare of the firm?

and (4) ask a few confidants, some colleagues, and even a former boss for their assessment of his political skills.

An Action Plan

The action system is similar to the action plans in the self-discipline model. Fred's action plan for becoming more politically astute might include reading books and articles about power and politics, listening to audiotapes, talking with people he considers politically astute, and developing a checklist of activities that he will engage in to acquire more power. Items on his political to-do list might include:

- Develop a list of the truly powerful people in my company who go beyond their position on the organizational chart.
- Develop contacts with these people. I'll volunteer to serve with them on task forces and high-status committees and use e-mail to stay in contact with them.
- Obtain vital information about the markets we serve and about what the competition is doing. I want to become valued for the information I have.
- Keep informed about company developments—to accomplish this I'll cultivate relationships with the right administrative assistants.

- Do what's necessary to help my boss succeed. If she looks good, I'll look good, and she will say good things about me to the right people.
- Show great loyalty to the company and my boss by being a good-mouther and defending my department when there's an interdepartmental dispute.
- Manage my impression so I appear successful and calm under pressure. I'll do what I can to speak in a convincing, articulate manner.
- Do what I can to be a good team player, giving the impression that I'm thinking first of the company and second of my career.
- Display leadership characteristics by being enthusiastic and listening carefully to people.

An action plan is worthless until set in motion. Planning it requires self-discipline—as does keeping it going. For example, Fred should keep a separate file or notebook with a schedule that lays out his action plan, linking one activity to the next.

Feedback on Actions

It's crucial to measure the effects of your actions against reality so that you can adjust your behavior accordingly. When your self-improvement goal is complex, such as career advancement, you will want to measure both the short- and long-term effectiveness of your actions. Long-term measures are important because self-improvement activities of major consequence have long-range implications. Cheryl, the international banking aspirant, won't know the career impact of taking additional courses on international currency until she becomes a successful international banking specialist.

Fred can determine how well he is learning political behavior by observing whether or not he is becoming better noticed by powerful people in his company. Fred has to be alert to any negative feedback suggesting that his actions are backfiring. He will know he needs to use more finesse if his boss says: "Fred, why are you kissing up to me so much? I find it disturbing."

Fred may need five or more years to know if his political self-improvement efforts have been truly successful. Among the success criteria he might use are his position in the organization, his income, and the respect he receives from a variety of people. To be more scientific, Fred should compare his progress with others of comparable education and experience who were at a similar level in the organization five years ago.

Wynton Marsalis, the jazz and classical trumpet player, has good insight into the importance of self-discipline to self-improvement and the importance of using a learning system. In lamenting the decline of jazz musicians, Marsalis says:

> Jazz has seldom been learned except by patient listening and practice. But no one practices much anymore. Nobody wants to do what's necessary to learn to play well—I mean learning what music in all its forms has to offer and then the long hours of practicing and improving. Youngsters today are too impatient.[2]

USING SELF-AWARENESS AND DOUBLE-LOOP LEARNING TO PROFIT FROM FEEDBACK

As you can see, feedback is an important source of information for self-improvement. Profiting from it, however, requires a high level of self-discipline in order to interpret its subtleties. Consider Arlene, who has lost three key group members over a six-month time span. She defensively dismissed the problem by saying, "I guess we just don't pay well enough to keep good people." Although the initial analysis might be correct, with a well-disciplined self-awareness orientation, however, she could dig deeper for reasons beyond the turnover: "Is there something in my leadership approach that creates turnover problems?" She might ask for the results of her staff's exit interviews, since they sometimes provide valuable information. People leaving the company are likely to be more candid about their experience than those still employed.

Noted organizational psychologist Chris Argyris has coined the terms "single-loop learning" and "double-loop learning" to differentiate between levels of self-awareness (see diagram below).[4] Single-loop learning is an easy, undisciplined approach, where learners seek minimum feedback that might substantially confront their basic ideas or actions. Like Arlene, single-loop learners think defensively. Argyris offers the example of a

Single-Loop Learning Versus Double-Loop Learning

thermostat that automatically turns on the heat whenever the room temperature drops below 68 degrees Fahrenheit (20 degrees Celsius).

Double-loop learning requires self-discipline. It is an in-depth type of learning that uses feedback to confront the validity of thinking in a given situation. For instance, a manager who has been included in a downsizing might say to himself, "Just rotten luck I guess. The company decided to cut costs, and my salary was pretty high." Another manager included in the downsizing might say, "I'm angry and sad that I was included in the downsizing. Why me? Ninety percent of company employees were not asked to leave. I'm going to find out why I wasn't considered valuable enough to retain."

SELF-DISCIPLINE IS THE UNDERLYING FORCE THAT ENABLES PEOPLE TO DEVELOP AND GROW SUBSTANTIALLY.

To achieve double-loop learning you must minimize defensive thinking. Argyris explains that a double-loop learning thermostat would ask, "Why am I set at 68 degrees?" and then ask whether another temperature might more economically achieve the goal of heating the room. Self-awareness and double-loop learning require a special application of self-discipline. You have to concentrate carefully on the meaning of feedback. Placed in a situation where the feedback could possibly be interpreted in more than one way, say to yourself: "My goal is to gain the edge in as many situations as possible. What message can I squeeze out of this situation? What is the environment telling me?"

RELATING PERSONAL IMPROVEMENT TO YOUR MISSION

If you'll remember, the first component of the self-discipline model is the mission statement. This is key to the success of any program.

A mission statement can be multipurpose. For instance, a mission statement can be effective in promoting self-improvement in your personal life. How many times have you given up on jogging or another exercise because your motivation just fizzled? The antidote is to understand how exercise supports your career mission. Physical fitness is an asset because it helps increase energy. Tom, a certified public accountant, gives his opinion on the subject:

> To me, self-discipline is the ability to do the things you need to do, even if you do not want to do those things. I need all the self-discipline I can find to run in the early morning hours—something I've been doing for five years. I would have given up on running four years ago, except that it helps my appearance.
>
> It gives a CPA an edge to look healthy and fresh. Each morning I come into the office looking healthy and fresh because of my running. My clients and the owner of my firm want me to look alert.

In short, if your self-improvement activity supports a clearly articulated mission, it is easier to stay focused. While engaging in a challenging self-improvement activity you are moving one step closer to your mission. If you are already achieving your mission, self-improvement activities can help them hold on to their gains.

You can probably see how the reality principle ties into being guided by a mission statement. Getting up early in the morning to run requires sacrificing the immediate pleasure of sleeping later or having a second cup of coffee. Yet, the long-term payoff from running each morning is much greater than the immediate gratification of sleeping later.

PROGRAMMING YOUR BRAIN FOR SELF-IMPROVEMENT

A basic self-improvement principle is that the thoughts you accept and keep are under your control. According to consultant Daniel

Araoz, until you accept this principle at a gut level, you are at the mercy of your own thoughts and maybe practicing *negative self-hypnosis* without even realizing what you are doing.[3]

Negative self-hypnosis occurs when you admit and retain negative thoughts that emphasize your fears, insecurities, disappointments, limitations, and anger. When you focus on negative thoughts you inhibit thoughts of your strengths, assets, inner resources, dreams, and ideals.

To combat negative self-hypnosis, you have to enter success thoughts into your brain. Araoz has developed a four-step process that is easy to learn and put into practice: *perception* of the negative thought; *interjection* of a positive thought; *pep talk* to yourself; and *ongoing benefits.*

Step One: You must become aware of your negative self-hypnosis (*perception*). Be sensitive to catching negative thoughts about yourself such as when you say, "I'm a fool," when all you have done is misplaced your keys.

Step Two: Halt negative input by substituting positive input (*interjection*). Forcing yourself not to think of a negative thought is not enough because it could become even more vivid in your mind. It is more effective to substitute a positive thought or visualize a pleasant experience just as the thought surfaces. Recall when you were at a peak moment of happiness such as getting a promotion or being on a romantic vacation. Recapture as many details as you can. It's useful to prepare a list of accomplishments in any area of your work or personal life so that when you encounter a negative thought you can substitute quickly. Choose one and mull over it in your mind as if you were looking at a scrapbook of your successes. Savor the thought for a while, and be aware of how good you feel.

Step Three: Reorient yourself through a *pep talk.* Remind yourself of a goal you had and how you achieved it. Reassure yourself by reviewing your strengths and assets. For example, "I know I can master serious photography because I'm good at operating high-tech equipment, and I have an artistic flair."

Another type of pep talk is to construct an oral version of a success vision. Imagine what it would be like to have your photos exhibited and what you would say to people who came to the exhibit.

Step Four: To achieve *ongoing benefits,* choose a short phrase that you can repeat to yourself many times over the next two or three days. The phrase can be as basic as, "I know how I want to improve, and I have the resources to do it."

By using the system of perception, interjection, pep talk, and ongoing benefits you will learn to control your thoughts, get away from negative self-hypnosis that might be blocking your well-intended efforts at self-improvement, and increase the probability that the payoff from self-improvement will be long lasting.

SELF-DEVELOPMENT OF WEAKNESSES

Today's euphemism for limitations or weaknesses is "developmental opportunity," because if you are deficient in some way you have an opportunity to develop. Overcoming weaknesses—or self-developing—is a matter of maintaining self-discipline and monitoring behavior. If you want to prevent a weakness from blocking your career progress or personal happiness, you have to take control of your own behavior. The definition of self-development offered by a team of researchers from the Center for Creative Leadership is right on target with my position: "By self-development we mean the conscious, deliberate effort to come to terms with one's limitations."[5]

To illustrate the nature of self-development, consider the weakness described by about 98 percent of people asked about their developmental needs: "I'm shy about public speaking." Asked what they are going to do to overcome this problem, about 95 percent say, "Take a course in public speaking." A public speaking course is certainly an effective beginning, but it does not create lasting changes in behavior. Overcoming shyness in public speaking will only take place when you apply self-discipline to practice the concepts learned in the course. The person really intent on becoming a better public speaker will search for—and even create—the chance to speak in front of a group.

Self-discipline also plays an important role in the continuous monitoring of one's behavior as the ensurer that the needed self-development occurs. After you identify a developmental need, it is necessary to periodically review your actions to be sure you are making the necessary improvements. Maria, a sales trainer, recognized the value of becoming a more colorful communicator. She enlisted her self-discipline to make the *conscious effort* to communicate more colorfully during training sessions. As part of her self-disciplined effort, Maria created a repertiore of sharp visual and auditory images of speaking in a lively and colorful manner.

On page 151 you'll find a list of a number of aspects of behavior that suggest a person needs improvement in interpersonal skills. Check each statement that is generally true for you. You can add to the reliability of this exercise by having one or two other people who know you well respond to these statements as they apply to you. Then compare your self-analysis with theirs.

COPING WITH AN ATTENTION DEFICIT DISORDER

A disorder that has been receiving a lot of attention from doctors, psychologists, teachers, and the people who suffer from it is Attention Deficit Disorder. ADD is an inherited neurobiological

BEHAVIORS CHECKLIST

Check

1. I'm too shy and reserved. _____
2. I bully and intimidate others too frequently. _____
3. I tell others what they want to hear rather than em- _____
phasizing the truth.
4. I have trouble expressing my feelings. _____
5. I make negative comments about people too readily. _____
6. Very few people pay attention to the ideas I con- _____
tribute during a meeting.
7. My personality isn't colorful enough. _____
8. People find me boring. _____
9. I pay too little attention to the meaning behind _____
what superiors and coworkers are saying.
10. It's very difficult for me to criticize others. _____
11. I'm too serious most of the time. _____
12. I avoid controversy in dealing with others. _____
13. I don't get my point across very well. _____
14. It's difficult for me to make small talk. _____
15. I boast too much about my accomplishments. _____
16. I strive too much for individual recognition instead _____
of looking for ways to credit the team.
17. Self-confidence is my weak point. _____
18. My spoken messages are too bland. _____
19. My written messages are too bland. _____
20. I read people poorly. _____
21. People take advantage of me because I'm too nice. _____
22. (Fill in your own statement.) _____

disorder that creates a brain imbalance. People with this syndrome have extreme difficulty concentrating. ADD first manifests itself as childhood hyperactivity; as the physical restlessness diminishes during puberty, the major remaining symptom is usually a short attention span. About 3 percent of both adults and children suffer from ADD.

In addition to people who have a genetically based Attention Deficit Disorder, many people develop similar symptoms in response to environmental pressures. A recent report on the subject concludes that "the ADD-type personality fits right into life in the high-tech, high-stim, fast-food, instant-gratification, short-attention-span, information-overloaded, overworked, media-saturated lifestyle that is America in the 1990s."[7] ADD also fits in with the lifestyle of many other industrial countries, including Canada, Japan, France, and Germany.

In addition to the short attention span, adults with ADD have a multitasking mind. Persons so afflicted have difficulty doing only one thing at a time. While watching television they balance checkbooks and converse with family members; while working at the computer they watch CNN Headline News; while reading a newspaper or magazine they work out on an exercise machine; while making love they drink wine and think about job problems.

Understanding your tendencies toward multitasking is an important first step in coping with Attention Deficit Disorder. The phenomenon of multitasking has been reframed in a way that is useful for self-improvement. Focusing on entirely one task at a time is the *monochronic* approach. In contrast, focusing on two or more activities at the same time is the *polychronic* approach.[8] People who start one task, then shift to another, then return to the original task are mildly polychronic. A much more polychronic approach would be to work on two or more tasks simultaneously.

You can measure your polychronicity by observing how many activities you typically carry out at the same time. Your subjective reactions to events are another indicator of polychronicity. Imagine that two different people are planning to write a report in the morning. Both begin writing, and after 45 minutes each receives a telephone call. Person A perceives the call as an interruption and attempts to reschedule the call for later in the afternoon. Person B answers the telephone, has a complete conversation, enjoys the break from the report, and returns to the report after the call.

Person A is relatively monochronic because she considers unscheduled events as negative interruptions that should be minimized and not allowed to disrupt scheduled activities. Person B is relatively polychronic because he perceives the telephone call as a normal part of the workday. The call should therefore receive as much attention as the report.

To measure your own tendency toward polychronicity, take the quiz on page 154. Based on a sample of working adults, the mean (average) score on their scale is 3.13, which you can use as a point of comparison for your own score.[9]

UNDERSTANDING YOUR TENDENCIES TOWARD MULTITASKING IS AN IMPORTANT FIRST STEP IN COPING WITH ATTENTION DEFICIT DISORDER.

How does understanding your tendency toward polychronicity (multitasking) help you cope with adult Attention Deficit Disorder? If you are strongly polychronic, you are off the hook somewhat. If this pattern has existed for many years, you can usually handle more than one task simultaneously without it being an indicator of ADD. Like many successful people, you can keep several different projects going at the same time. You can still be a self-disciplined person and pay some attention to a second task if you are a true polychronic.

Let's return now to the problem of the person who has a culturally induced Attention Deficit Disorder that makes it exceedingly difficult to concentrate on self-improvement. Milton wants to study information about overcoming shyness but can only read a

POLYCHRONIC ATTITUDE INDEX

Please circle how you feel about the following statements. Circle your choice on the scale provided: strongly agree (SA), agree (A), neutral (N), disagree (D), or strongly disagree (SD).

	SD	D	N	A	SA
1. I do not like to juggle several activities at the same time.	5	4	3	2	1
2. People should not try to do many things at once.	5	4	3	2	1
3. When I sit down at my desk, I work on one project at a time.	5	4	3	2	1
4. I am comfortable doing several things at the same time.	1	2	3	4	5

Add up your points, and divide the total by 4. Then plot your score on the scale below.

1.0	1.5	2.0	2.5	3.0	3.5	4.0	4.5	5.0
Monochronic								Polychronic

The lower your score (below 3.0) the more monochronic your orientation, and the higher your score (above 3.0) the more polychronic.

few lines before becoming distracted. The recommended antidote is to force concentration in small increments.

For instance, Milton might read five lines at a sitting one hour and return to read six lines several hours later. The next day, the reading segment is upped to two paragraphs, followed by three paragraphs the next day. Continuing forward, Milton adds another paragraph the next day. (FlashRead, a successful computer program designed to improve concentration, is based on the same principle. It improves reading concentration by quickly flashing successive segments of sentences.) Should Milton reach a stage where the amount of reading is more than he can do without being distracted, he reverts back to a doable amount of reading.

As basic as this tactic may sound, it is the way self-discipline in general strengthens. With one brick at a time you build an edifice of a focused mind that enables you to capture the transformational power of self-discipline.

CHAPTER 8

OVERCOMING COUNTER- PRODUCTIVE HABITS

When counterproductive habits are sapping your energy, hurting your productivity, or interfering with your personal relationships, self-discipline can be the vehicle for getting back on track. A counterproductive habit (or behavior pattern) is a recurring activity that blocks your achieving important goals. Well-known counterproductive habits include procrastination, substance abuse, food abuse, compulsive gambling, compulsive shopping, absenteeism, tardiness, and promiscuity. People are remarkably inventive in developing idiosyncratic forms of counterproductive behavior. Some people clip their fingernails during business meetings; others swear at and belittle subordinates. I know one manager who regularly submits his expense reports so late he often misses the deadline for reimbursement.

Can such dreadful habits as these realistically be controlled through self-discipline and self-control? Of course, I believe so. And many have proven it possible. Think about the people you know—and perhaps yourself—who exercise self-discipline to control their counterproductive habits. Take cigarette smoking. Limiting, if not eliminating, this habit provides a revealing example of how exercising self-discipline can affect a bad habit.

Smokers make decisions about where and when to smoke because the law prohibits smoking or because there are times or situations *they* feel are unsuited for smoking. (Even during the heyday of smoking almost nobody smoked in houses of worship, the subways, or while visiting an office in which no ashtrays were present.) For instance, a smoker may decide that smoking is okay during dessert but not the main course, in his or her own car, but not in somebody else's.

Wanting to overcome a counterproductive habit means you are being guided by the reality principle and want to experience long-term satisfaction. (Most counterproductive habits provide short-term gratification.) But how self-discipline and the reality principle intercept and curb counterproductive behavior can be affected by your perception of the behavior itself.

A DISEASE OR A BAD HABIT?

A major controversy about the nature of counterproductive behavior is whether it is a disease or a maladaptive habit. The difference is more than philosophical, because it determines how much self-discipline you believe you can exert to overcome and prevent problems. If you perceive counterproductive behavior to be a disease, you will exercise less ownership of the problem and tend to look for others to help you cure your disease. In contrast, if you perceive counterproductive behavior to be a maladaptive habit, you are likely to believe you have the power to control the problem.

The controversy about disease versus bad habits is pointedly illustrated by alcohol abuse. A person's approach to overcoming alcohol abuse depends to some extent on whether he regards alcoholism as a disease or as maladaptive behavior. That alcoholism is a disease is the majority viewpoint among mental health specialists and the general public. According to Jeffrey Lynn Speller, Harvard Medical School psychiatrist:

> **IF YOU PERCEIVE COUNTERPRODUCTIVE BEHAVIOR TO BE A DISEASE, YOU WILL EXERCISE LESS OWNERSHIP OF THE PROBLEM.**
>
> The central premise of the disease concept of alcohol is that the alcoholic cannot control his or her drinking—one drink usually leads in time to twenty. Alcoholism is a chronic, long-term disease over which one has no control and which has an inevitable downhill course. There is no cure except to stop drinking—completely and for good. . . . An alcoholic can no more control his or her drinking than a diabetic can control the malfunctioning of the pancreas.[1]

People who regard alcoholism as a disease are likely to seek medical or psychological help. To conquer it they seek help from a physician or counselor, either through outpatient visits to a mental health practitioner or at a clinic for substance abusers. Someone with severe alcoholism might volunteer to become an inpatient at a hospital specializing in alcoholism treatment. (In many instances, medical intervention of this type is the only workable alternative because alcoholism has gone beyond the realm of self-control.)

Others view alcoholism as a self-defeating, counterproductive behavior under a person's control. People who accept the bad habit view of alcohol abuse might seek professional assistance with their problem; yet the thrust of their efforts is to discipline themselves to change their counterproductive ways. Looking upon alcoholism as maladaptive behavior runs contrary to groups such as Alcoholics Anonymous, which labels alcoholism as a sickness over which the victim has no control. They therefore insist on abstinence.

In contrast to the Alcohol Anonymous position, many experts believe that alcoholics can and do moderate their drinking. They consider the likelihood of relapse greater if the recovering alcohol abuser thinks that craving and loss of control are inevitable. They consider equally harmful the belief that a single drink leads to uncontrollable drinking. At scientific conferences on alcoholism treatment, a return to social drinking is thought to be a realistic goal.[2]

A person who believes that alcohol abuse is under his or her control can, exercising self-discipline, take the following precautions to prevent a major drinking problem:[3]

- Limit the consumption of alcoholic beverages to three on any given day, but average no more than two per day.
- Abstain from alcoholic beverages for at least two consecutive days each week.
- Drink only standard-size beverages: 1 ounce of whiskey in a mixed drink; 12 ounces of beer; or 5 ounces of wine.
- No drinking on an empty stomach.
- Drink slowly and intersperse alcoholic beverages with nonalcoholic beverages.
- When faced with the urge for an alcoholic beverage, substitute a glass of fruit juice or water.
- Make friends with people whose social life does not revolve around drinking alcoholic beverages. Associate with responsible drinkers.

• Regard drinking before 6:00 p.m. as a personal taboo.

The above suggestions imply that mature adults can exercise the self-discipline to enjoy moderate alcohol consumption without falling prey to alcohol abuse. The same suggestions can be used to convert problem drinking into relatively safe drinking.

AN OVERVIEW OF THE PROGRAM FOR SELF-DIRECTED CHANGE

Self-directed change has been studied and experimented with for over thirty years. Enough reliable information on the topic exists to provide effective guides for overcoming counterproductive behavior. Before I present the details of a process of self-directed change I'd like you to ponder the following version of one of the most overused jokes in circulation:

Question: "How many psychologists does it take to change a light bulb?"

Answer: "None, if the light bulb wants to change."

Overused? Yes, but this joke carries two subtle messages. First, if you are not motivated to change, it will be difficult for an external change agent to bring about changes. Second, most change is self-change. Even if you seek professional help for counterproductive behavior, the professional can only guide you. It is *you* who must translate your new insights and understanding into lasting changes. For example, suppose a person receives medication to help control the tension that is prompting him to bite his nails. He may be calmer, but he has to exercise the self-discipline to not bite his nails when faced with work and personal pressures.[4]

Model for Self-Directed Change

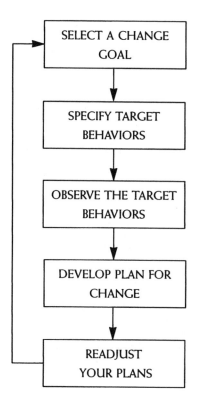

Take a look at the flowchart above, which illustrates a program for overcoming counterproductive behavior. Now, let's dig into the implementation details.

Select a Change Goal

The first step is to select a counterproductive behavior creating problems for you in work, personal life, or both. Perhaps you have received frequent feedback on repetitive behavior of yours that irritates other people. Maybe you have been making New Year's resolutions about the same behavior for many years, but no permanent change has been forthcoming. Have you engaged in impulsive behavior that has gotten you into trouble too many times? Here is a sampling of counterproductive habits others have chosen as a change goal:

- Absenteeism and lateness
- Abuse of power (such as misappropriation of company resources)
- Alcohol abuse
- Anger outbursts at the wrong time and place
- Attention seeking in the form of hogging center stage during meetings
- Blaming others for your problems
- Bridge burning
- Choking under pressure
- Commitment breaking
- Compulsive gambling
- Compulsive sex
- Compulsive spending
- Confrontation avoidance
- Deception and lying
- Delegation refusal
- Drug abuse
- Eating disorder
- Excuse making
- Grammatical errors to the point of appearing unintelligent
- Indecisiveness
- Insulting others and their ideas
- Modesty to an excessive degree
- Negativism at home and on the job
- Political insensitivity
- Procrastination
- Shyness and timidity
- Snooping into other people's files

- Stealing from others
- Swearing excessively in inappropriate settings
- Workaholism to the point that not working is painful

Selecting a goal involves specifying behaviors in particular situations that you would like to change. Using a general label, or trait, as a change goal lacks the specificity necessary to tell you what behavior to change.

Laura, a manager at a hair products company, says her problem is that she is too insulting. "Too insulting" communicates a general meaning but does not pinpoint behaviors that require change. The program of self-change being presented requires specificity. To move beyond identifying a trait that you have to change, translate this trait into concrete examples from work and personal life. Laura, who would like to become less insulting to people, develops the list of behavioral specifics on page 164.

Specify Target Behaviors

Specifying the behaviors you are attempting to change is the logical next step after having specified goals. A major premise of self-directed change is that you need to understand the behaviors you would be engaging in if you reached your goal. An effective way of doing this is to *ask yourself what you would be doing if you achieved your goal.* If your goal was to overcome alcohol abuse, you might list a behavior such as, "Attend a reception and enjoy two drinks without having an overwhelming compulsion to keep drinking." Just as examples of goals are concrete, so are the specifications of behavior indicating the goal has been reached.

Laura specified the behaviors she would engage in that would enable her to get her point across without hurling insults. (Compare these statements to Laura's list of insults on the next page.) For instance:

- "I would tell my assistant that her nice features would be showcased to advantage if she chose a few more of the right outfits."
- "I would tell my neighbor that her newborn had distinctive features similar to those I saw of an infant in a movie."
- "I would tell my husband that he was a good competitor both as a golfer and a lover."

To sharpen your list of behaviors that need changing, keep a log of critical events and how you reacted in terms of the behavior you want to change. Laura had a rich list of past insults she hurled

---

SELF-DIRECTED CHANGE WORKSHEET

Examples of Insults I Have Delivered
On the Job

1. Told my manager he had a 1960s mentality.
2. Told the vice president of marketing that our product line is embarrassingly bad.
3. Told my assistant that she looks frumpy.
4. Said to one of my group members that he's not smart enough to get promoted.

Off the Job

1. Told my neighbor that her newborn looked like he was from the Planet of the Apes.
2. Said to my husband jokingly that his golf swing was better than his love making.
3. Offered my honest opinion to a friend that she should get a breast reduction.
4. Told my children that I was glad they were just average kids, so in this way people don't expect too much from them.

---

at people. But for several days, she looked critically at any situation in which an opportunity existed to be insulting, and jotted down her responses. One day when she went grocery shopping, the cashier placed a loaf of bread under a six pack of beer. Laura wrote later, "I really slammed into the kid. I told him that if he had passed a course in high-school physics he would know that cans of beer are denser than a loaf of bread. This is just the type of insult I'm trying to overcome."

By using self-discipline to observe your behavior, the process of change has already begun. Since the reason you are recording your behavior is to improve, you will probably begin to behave in a manner consistent with your goals.

Another facet of observing your target behaviors is to examine what is happening when you're not achieving your goal (acting the way you would like to act). Analyze the chain of events that precede your behavior. A person whose problem is overeating might observe that he eats too much when he is restless. A man engaged in a self-directed change program noted:

> I notice that when I'm waiting for somebody in a bar or hotel lobby I feel uneasy. One night I was meeting some friends at 7:00 at a bar. They didn't show up until 7:20. Like a hog, I kept going back to the free appetizer tray. I must have eaten ten Swedish meatballs in the 20 minutes I was waiting. I also had two beers. I know if they had showed up on time, I would not have binged.

Laura noticed that she was most apt to hurl an insult when she was under time pressure. For example, "When I told Jeff (the group member) that he was not smart enough to get promoted, I was trying to end the performance evaluation session. We had already gone over the time I had budgeted for the meeting. My next appointment was waiting. I guess that when I'm in a rush, I have to be on guard to bite my tongue."

To strengthen your understanding of how you would be acting if you achieved your goal, select an appropriate model. Laura identified a work associate she perceived to be diplomatic and supportive rather than insulting, and observed how he communicates criticism or disagreement without being insulting: "When Ralph [her boss] was talking about a group member who wasn't promotable, he said the person needed to improve her *analytical skills*. I guess this would give the person a hook to work with rather than saying she wasn't bright enough. That could be devastating to her ego."

At this point you have established a change goal, specified target behaviors, and observed your target behaviors. You are now ready to specify your goals as counterproductive behavior in a situation that you want to decrease. An alternative is to specify a productive behavior in a situation that you want to increase.

Before moving on to the next step, complete the description of your own problem behavior in a situation.[5]

My goal is to increase _____ in
(behavior)

_____ .
(situation)

Focusing on *productive* behavior, Laura, the insulting manager, stated:

My goal is to increase *diplomacy and tact* in *situations in which I am under time pressure.*

Focusing on *counterproductive* behavior, she stated:

My goal is to decrease *insulting others* in *situations in which I am under time pressure.*

The words "increase" and "decrease" are carefully chosen. Self-directed change is based on behavior modification, a method that attempts to decrease the frequency of some behaviors and increase the frequency of others. It makes no realistic promises of a 100-percent cure. If you believe that the appropriate application of self-discipline and self-control can help you ameliorate a situation, you will not be *fearful* of ever having a relapse. If, however, instead you believe that success means never again engaging in the smallest incident of counterproductive behavior, you will be setting yourself up for failure and disappointment.

Develop a Plan for Change

Your plan for change is the heart of the program for self-control. The self-discipline model also contains a plan for change referred to as "develop action plans to achieve goals." The plan for change here contains both action plans and a behavioral contract with yourself for administering self-chosen rewards and punishments.

ACTION PLANS

The most practical action plan involves carefully monitoring your behavior and then consciously stopping the counterproductive habit at the point at which it is most likely to surface. If your counterproductive habit is to lose important items when you are rushed, you would force yourself to take 30 seconds to say: "Right now I'm rushed, so I have to be careful. I am quite likely to misplace my keys, my wallet, or forget where I parked my car. Instead of messing up again, I'm going to be careful to put my keys back in the same place. My wallet is secure here in my pocket (or handbag). I'm parked in section K-11. I'll write that down in my appointment calendar."

This approach can work for much more serious counterproductive behavior. An engineer was accused by two women in his office of sexual harassment. The specific charge was that he brushed against them on several occasions while conducting work. After investigating the charges, the company placed the man on probation and offered him counseling. His action plan developed during counseling was to use the *stop response*. When working in close proximity to a woman, he would say to himself: "Stop, you're in the danger zone now. Have a nice little fantasy, but that's it. Uninvited touching is sexual harassment." Despite his continued fantasy life, the engineer was able to control his overt counterproductive (and illegal and immoral) behavior.

Although your primary action plan involves self-discipline and behavior self-monitoring, it is helpful to supplement the plan with other interventions. Self-discipline is used to implement the insight and skills you acquire from the intervention.

Laura, who was struggling to control her insults, attended a seminar about the art of effective criticism and met with a mental health specialist about her habit of insulting others. All of the insights she gained were incorporated into her action plan. Unless self-discipline is applied to implementing the new insights, no changes will occur.

Self-control programs require that people attempting to change their behavior administer their own rewards and punishment for progress or lack of progress. The term behavioral contract refers to the idea that you reach an agreement with yourself as to how you will reward and punish yourself.

Preparing and implementing a behavioral contract places you in the self-discipline mode. The contract communicates the insight that you are responsible for controlling your own counterproductive behavior. Preparing a behavioral contract is a struggle for many people because it clashes with the traditional mental set that rewards and punishments are administered only by a second party. Whoever heard of grounding yourself or giving yourself a recognition pin?

To carry out your behavioral contract, three components are needed: a log of your behaviors (which you are already keeping), a list of potential rewards, and a list of potential punishments. Your log can be maintained mentally, but a notebook is more effective considering the foibles of human memory.

In choosing rewards and punishments for your behavioral contract, remember they will actually have to be administered; your choices have to be deliverable by you. A two-week tour of Alaska might be a nice reward for not overeating at a party, but do you have the time and money? Suspending yourself from driving during a weekend might be a powerful punishment, but you might become angry enough to drop your program of controlling how you eat.

Use your imagination and personal preferences in choosing rewards for your self-control program. As a starting point, consider reinforcers others have used:

- taking a long bath
- buying yourself a small gift
- eating a favorite meal or snack
- making love during the day
- going to the beach
- playing your favorite sport an extra day during the week
- spending more time at a favorite hobby
- purchasing a book, tape, or CD
- playing computer games for 3 hours
- drinking champagne at 2:00 in the morning
- dining at a favorite restaurant
- taking off for an entire day without being accountable to anyone
- pampering yourself in a way you like to be pampered
- visiting an art museum
- attending a rock concert

- watching a sporting event or soap opera for 3 hours
- scheduling an extra session with a hair stylist

Punishments should play a smaller role in your behavioral contract than rewards because punishment has several key limitations.[6] One is that counterproductive behavior is already a form of self-punishment. When Laura insulted work associates, loved ones, and friends she received punishment in the form of rejection.

Another problem with punishment is that alone it does not teach new behavior. Punishing yourself for being late for a meeting is not as effective as rewarding yourself for doing the right thing—being prompt. Punishment carries a third problem: It may engender resentment and hostility. Suppose you punish yourself by throwing away your tickets to a play or sporting event. You would most likely sulk during the time the event takes place.

In short, self-administered punishment has a role in your behavioral contract, but mostly as a supplement to your program of self-administered rewards. Here is a sampling of punishments for your behavioral contract:

- declaring a two-week moratorium from your favorite hobby
- declaring a two-week moratorium from your favorite alcoholic beverage
- depriving yourself of any of the rewards on your list
- cleaning up debris in your neighborhood instead of watching television
- reading the least favorite section of your newspaper every day for one week
- cleaning and scraping the underside of your car

For maximum effect, administer your rewards and punishments close to the time in which the right or wrong behavior occurred. Suppose Laura's boss enters her office at 9:15 Monday morning mostly to chat about weekend events. Being goal-oriented, Laura might want to say, "Don't you have anything more important to do than rehash your weekend?" Ugh! An insult delivered straight to the boss's solar plexus. Instead, Laura who has been working on her diplomacy skills, says, "Is it possible to continue this discussion at lunch time? I'm intent on getting this analysis done so I can meet the timetable you have given me." Great. Laura has diplomatically explained to her boss that she is busy working on his problem, so they will have to chat later.

Proud of her tactfulness in a situation that would have provoked insults in the past, Laura decides to reward herself. After work she buys herself a bottle of a new cologne she had been curious about. At midnight, she tries out the cologne to see what effect it has on her husband (a double reward).

Another issue to consider is what to do when the behavioral contract you have prepared for yourself is not doing the job—your counterproductive behavior continues unabated. One antidote is to keep trying harder and at the same time, increase the intensity of the rewards. Increasing the intensity of your punishments is another possibility. Yet because of the limitations of punishments already discussed, intensifying punishments could backfire.

PUNISHING YOURSELF FOR BEING LATE FOR A MEETING IS NOT AS EFFECTIVE AS REWARDING YOURSELF FOR DOING THE RIGHT THING—BEING PROMPT.

If your program of self-directed change is not producing results within sixty days despite having followed most of the prescriptions above, you may require external intervention. Possibly you need further insight into understanding why you persist in self-defeating behavior. Professional help may give you the insights necessary to unblock your program of self-directed change.

An overweight woman was failing in her program of weight reduction through self-directed change. A few counseling sessions helped her realize she was afraid of losing weight. Her concern was that if she lost weight, she would attract men for superficial reasons only. Her counselor helped her realize that she had enough intuition to enable her to weed out men who were attracted to women primarily because of their physical shape. The woman then returned to her weight-loss program and achieved her weight-loss goal within four months.

Readjust Your Plans

A program of self-control should be flexible. Exercising self-discipline does not mean that you are so singly focused on your goal that it is immutable. A self-disciplined person is prepared to fine-tune or change goals if circumstances warrant it. As you embark upon your program of self-change, you will see new possibilities in your own behavior as well as in the situation. Goals may change in response to changes in the environment. When the situation changes, the self-disciplined person does not become less persistent. Instead, she pursues another target with vigor.

Herb, an industrial sales representative, illustrates constructive goal changing during a self-change program. Being basically a shy person, Herb realized he established poor eye contact with existing and prospective customers. He chose the goal of improved eye contact because he thought failing to do so was counterproductive. Herb carried out many of the techniques involved in self-directed change. Using self-discipline, along with watching videotapes of successful sales techniques, Herb improved his eye contact. However, neither his rapport with customers nor his sales increased substantially.

One day an irritated customer said to Herb, "You're not listening again." Herb asked the customer what she meant by the comment. The customer replied, "I can't imagine that dozens of people haven't told you that you have poor listening skills. You have such good product knowledge, if you combined it with careful listening you would double your sales."

This time Herb *was* listening. His new self-change goal was to become a more active listener. Herb struggled to improve his listening skills, and the struggle paid large dividends as his closing ratio increased.

CASE HISTORY OF A DRAMATIC WEIGHT LOSS

Angela Vitello, dressed in black leggings and a clingy V-neck sweater, holds up what she used to wear.[7] The suburban woman stretches a pair of pale green shorts across her trim torso. A single leg opening looks large enough to encompass both her thighs with room to spare. Then the 38-year-old holds up a tentlike print sundress, her head poking up behind the unfurling fabric.

> A SELF-DISCIPLINED PERSON IS PREPARED TO FINE-TUNE OR CHANGE GOALS IF CIRCUMSTANCES WARRANT IT.

When I spoke to Vitello she was eager to share her accomplishments with others so they too could overcome crippling habits. "If I tell someone I lost 280 pounds, he or she wants proof," says Vitello, a size 12 who once scoured the racks at specialty stores to find size 52 clothes. She brings out photos of the last three years that show the 5-foot-4-inch woman gradually shrinking from 425 pounds to 145, before settling at 150.

One of those "before" pictures is glued to the wallet-sized pack that holds her Deal-A-Meal cards. She has used these menu planners for three years. That's when she embarked on the eating plan of Richard Simmons, the fitness guru. Vitello says that the cards helped her develop the self-discipline she needed. "Just moving the cards gave me a start in becoming self-disciplined": Choosing cards from the menu planner became her daily goal.

Since losing the weight, Vitello has become a disciple of Simmons, patron saint of bathroom-scale watchers. Before-and-after photographs of her are on the box containing the

Deal-A-Meal cards and videos. She also has done a commercial for the weight-loss plan. Vitello now runs a daycare center from her home and also sells Avon products.

Vitello says she has received many of Simmons's inspirational messages. "Whenever I have a bad day, I either see Richard on TV or he calls." (Simmons is an important role model and source of emotional support for Vitello.)

She sits at the round table in her kitchen and talks about the exalted status food held for her Italian family. At Christmas, for example, Vitello used to bake pies, cakes, and 137 dozen cookies. "Now I have the self-discipline to not sample so much of what I cook. I didn't in the past. My daily goal is 1,400 calories, no more. My reward is liking my body."

In the past, people would ask Vitello, "How could you let yourself get that way?" My answer is you don't let yourself. It doesn't happen overnight. But one day, there it is.

Vitello kept denying just how heavy she had become, saying she weighed only 280 pounds when she knew she was well over 300. She says she knew she was cheating her two children out of the activities other kids enjoyed with their parents. She was finally confronted with the truth. At a family picnic, an aunt she had not seen in several years told Angela she was concerned about her weight. The woman, also overweight, said she didn't want her niece to be a victim of the family history of heart trouble.

"She made me say I was fat and out of control," Vitello recalls. The next day Vitello began to take control of her life. Just before she was ready to eat the picnic leftovers for breakfast, her mother, Frances Arena, called and asked what Angela was doing. When she heard the answer, there was silence.

After hanging up, Vitello dug out the Deal-A-Meal menu cards she'd bought months before. (These cards facilitate the exercise of self-control and self-directed change.) "My heart and mind came together," Vitello says. "My pastor says you can't deal with sin

174

until you've had enough. Obesity is a sin. I'd had enough. . . . The Lord gave me a lot of grace in this," says Vitello. "I went through nineteen months and didn't cheat once. (Observe the strict self-discipline.) The Lord gave me the strength, and he gave me Richard to show me how."

Vitello says Deal-A-Meal is like the food pyramid introduced by the Department of Agriculture in 1992, allowing more grains and fewer fats. "But Richard was way ahead of the government," she says. By following the plan and walking for exercise, Vitello lost more than 150 pounds within seven months, when she wrote Simmons. (Following Deal-A-Meal and exercise constituted Vitello's action plan.)

"I never poured out to people what was in my heart." She had never told anyone how much it hurt to be called Hippo or Mama Cass, or how hard it was to work up any self-esteem, even though she knew inside she was a worthwhile person. In her letter Vitello told Simmons about her progress. He answered, and that correspondence led to television appearances and commercials. Yet Vitello insists that pride in her accomplishments is the driving force in doing commercials about weight loss. (Remember the importance of enjoyment of the task itself for achieving self-discipline?)

While many family members cannot remember her at 425 pounds, says Vitello, a 425-pound person still lurks inside. "I told Richard I used to be a thin person trapped in a fat body. Now I'm a fat person trapped in a thin body."

Vitello says that by taking her life back, she has more to give her family. "I am much more of a wife and mother." But sometimes when she catches sight of her reflection, she's not sure who she sees. I have to fight in my head. "You're not 425 pounds anymore."

Vitello's program of self-directed change has taken a new direction. She explains that she must now muster the self-discipline to exercise enough to tone her body. (In self-directed change, plans can be readjusted.) Vitello feels that during the weight-loss program she developed exceptional ability to control her own behavior. She can now apply this same ability to meet new challenges.

SELF-
CONTROL OF
STRESS

How many people do you know suffering from an uncomfortable level of stress who choose one of the dozens of scientifically sound and clinically proven approaches to stress management, from stress-management programs to home exercise machines? How many of these same people continue to suffer from an agonizing amount of negative stress?

Many people who begin programs of stress management with good intentions fail to use the insights and techniques the program offers. More books, articles, and cassette programs about stress management are tossed aside after brief exposure than read thoroughly—and referred to regularly.

Managing stress is a major challenge for which the appropriate application of self-discipline can make the difference between success and failure. Without effective application of self-discipline, stress is exceedingly difficult to control. A clinical psychologist provides this perspective on self-discipline and stress management:

> In recent years, our group has worked with thousands of corporate employees who have either been laid off or face the sword of Damascus. The patients who get long-term relief from their stress are those who actively involve themselves in solving their own problems. The patients who listen to our advice but make no commitment to necessary changes find no permanent symptom relief. They still suffer because they just don't get around to making necessary changes in their thinking and behavior.

A research study conducted with college students in Canada also found that self-discipline facilitates reducing stress. The students who were unable to reduce stress generally blamed the problem on lack of time and lack of self-discipline.[1]

I would like to introduce you to a handful of self-discipline-based approaches to bringing stress under control. The techniques are presented in sufficient detail so you can mobilize self-discipline to both relieve symptoms and make positive changes in your life. They are related to the self-discipline model because they are action plans for the goal of stress reduction. I recommend that you choose one or two of the techniques presented that best fit your personal style and preferences. And remember: look for the fun within stress-management activities.

CONFRONTATION AND PROBLEM SOLVING

Self-control of stress begins with confrontation. You exert self-discipline to acknowledge that there is a problem for which a solution must be found. You then attack the problem head on, and push doggedly toward your goal. I am not dismissing the importance of understanding why you perceive a particular situation as stressful. You may also need to calm yourself down emotionally so you can begin to attack your problems rationally. Yet until you have the discipline to really work on the problem that is creating your stress symptoms, it will resurface periodically.

After you identify what you think is the true stressor (the cause of the stress), follow the steps in problem solving and decision making: Clarify the problem, identify the alternatives, weigh the alternatives, and then select one alternative. The story of Louise, a small-business owner, will help explain the confrontation and problem-solving approach to stress reduction:

Suffering from an uncomfortable level of stress, Louise blamed it on "all the horribly steep taxes self-employed people have to pay." Louise explained that she usually didn't have enough money left over to pay taxes, and so was typically behind schedule especially for the quarterly estimated taxes.

Since the government only asks people to pay taxes on money they have earned, I asked Louise what happened to the government's share? Louise replied that she had so many other bills to pay that she did a poor job of holding back the government's share. She also sometimes spent the money she was supposed to send to the government to pay social security taxes.

As a result of being delinquent on taxes, Louise faced several stressors. She sometimes had to borrow money to pay taxes, and the government imposed stiff interest penalties. In addition, she had to worry about her business generating enough cash to cover these extra expenses.

I encouraged Louise to look at several alternatives that would get her tax stress under control. One was to sell or disband her business, which she found overwhelmingly stressful. She couldn't imagine attempting to get out of one business and look for a job at the same time. Besides, one of the reasons Louise chose self-employment was that she perceived working for others as stressful.

Another alternative was to systematically and deliberately set aside the government's share of revenue as she received money from customers. This seemed to make sense. Louise opened a money market fund just for taxes; whenever she deposited business receipts, she deposited approximately 30 percent into her tax fund. To begin the new system, Louise made adroit use of self-talk. She told herself repeatedly, "Only about 70 percent of business receipts is actually my money. If I were employed by a large firm, the employer would be deducting withholding tax. I am my own employer. I do the withholding."

Louise found withholding the appropriate amount of tax money to be painful at first. When it came time to send estimated and social security taxes to the government, however, Louise was relaxed instead of stressed. Although not happy about paying taxes—Who is?—she was no longer in a panic. Louise had attacked the major contributor to her job stress.

MEDITATION

Meditation is one of the oldest methods of reducing stress. It enables you to take control of the physiological responses that accompany a stressor. When you meditate properly, your stress symptoms are under control. Furthermore, you calm yourself down sufficiently so your tolerance for potentially stressful situations increases substantially. The Indian gurus who developed transcendental meditation (TM) were known for their self-discipline.

If you want to exercise self-control over your physiological responses, such as breathing and heart rate, TM is ideal. Remember though, you must still confront the real stressors facing you. TM is effective because it may put you in the right frame of mind to solve significant problems.

Transcendental meditation is easy to use because it has few rigid guidelines.[2] You practice it for about 20 to 30 minutes per day, twice a day. The recommended times for meditating are right before breakfast and right before dinner. During meditation take a seated position on a bed, carpeted floor, or floor cushion. The lotus position, or "physical centeredness," is preferred. When in the lotus position your hands touch each other, with fingers extended. To place your hands properly, imagine yourself praying. Cross your legs with the criss-cross occurring at the ankles. The lotus position is known to be the most relaxed of any seated position.

Close your eyes and keep the room free of any other possible sensory distractions. Find a word or sound to use as a personal mantra, something short and relaxing to pronounce, such as "umm," or "lam," or "on." Repeat your mantra over and over. Mental focusing of this type prevents you from thinking about problems or material objects. Using a mantra is yet another form of the visual focusing so necessary for self-discipline.

Meditation is not for everybody, however. Some people are too impatient and too focused on work and personal goals to feel comfortable taking the time to meditate. If you are like this, I advise you to combine confrontation and problem solving with several of the everyday methods of relaxation described below. Although these relaxation methods still require self-discipline to practice regularly, they are less ritualistic than meditation.

THE THOUGHT-STOPPING TECHNIQUE

A major step forward in reducing stress through self-discipline is to increase your awareness of stress signals in your body. Stress manifests itself in various ways:[3]

- *Physical* symptoms include upset stomach, increased heart-beat and breathing rate, chest pains, muscle aches and pains.
- *Cognitive* symptoms include decreased alertness, difficulties in concentration, forgetfulness, and careless mistakes.
- *Emotional* symptoms include tension, short temper, boredom, mental and physical fatigue, and feelings of hopelessness.
- *Behavioral* symptoms include agitation, restlessness, major changes in eating habits, and substance abuse.

This list is but a sampling of stress symptoms. It is important that you discipline yourself to identify your particular reactions to stressors. Take note of and record their intensity as well as the time of the day when they occur. You may find that the mere act of recording your symptoms reduces their incidence, because once you realize you are beginning to take control of your health, the process of change begins.

After you have increased your sensitivity to the stress symptoms, the next step is to identify *what* and *how* you were thinking and feeling just before you felt stressed. Stress usually stems from your interpretation and perception of an event, not the event itself. One person might experience stress when confronted with a backlog of fifty e-mail messages. Another might interpret those messages as a source of playful, pleasant activity.

What typically triggers stress reactions is your own stream of negative thoughts, such as: "I will waste half my day responding to these messages" or "Why do all these people have to monopolize my time with e-mail messages?" The negative thoughts in the brain stimulate sympathetic nervous system activity, which in turn leads to physiological stress reactions, like increased heart rate, elevated blood pressure, shortness of breath, and increased perspiration.

To gain control over negative stress you must learn how to terminate unproductive, worrisome thoughts. Thought-stopping will accomplish this end. Choose either the term "stop" or "cancel," and quietly but emphatically repeat it whenever you engage in anxiety-provoking thought. When first dealing with a disturbing thought, you may need to invoke thought-stopping 50 to 100 times per day.

Joel tried this technique when he began experiencing considerable stress because his girlfriend left him for another man. He became preoccupied with thoughts of her. For example, whenever he got into his car, all he thought of was his former girlfriend seated next to him. Whenever he opened a bottle of wine he remembered pouring wine for her first at dinner.

Initially Joel used thought-stopping about ten times per hour. After several months, he would think of his former girlfriend only occasionally. (Joel had also confronted the problem by dealing with his loneliness: He found another girlfriend who had much to offer.)

> A MAJOR STEP FORWARD IN REDUCING STRESS THROUGH SELF-CONTROL IS TO INCREASE YOUR AWARENESS OF STRESS SIGNALS IN YOUR BODY.

Thought-stopping can also be used to substitute rational for irrational thoughts. For instance, during a steady downturn in the stock market a person might become preoccupied with the irrational thought that all her investments will be wiped out. She should stop and say, "Nonsense, I have a diversified portfolio. History suggests that if you have diversified investments and hold on for the long term, the value of your investments will increase."

Self-discipline is required for thought-stopping because you have to focus your mind to act quickly when negative or irrational thoughts surface. This is not easy to do because most of us have a tendency to ruminate over problems, and think of extremely negative scenarios. Yet with practice, you can learn to use self-control to overcome worrisome thoughts. Try thought-stopping tomorrow on your most troublesome, recurring thought.

PROGRESSIVE MUSCLE RELAXATION

A potent technique for using self-control to reduce stress is to relax your muscles. A major premise underlying the muscle relaxation technique is that you cannot be both relaxed and tense at the same time. If you place yourself in a relaxed state, your tension will disappear. As in meditation, when you are relaxed your body is calmed down, not revved up. You are prepared for peace, not for battle. The relaxed state is also the building up or constructive process of the body. Fortunately, it is within the power of most people to achieve this beneficial state of relaxation.

EACH TIME YOU OBSERVE YOURSELF STARTING TO TIGHTEN UP IN SOME PART OF YOUR BODY OR TO SHORTEN YOUR BREATHING, TELL YOURSELF THAT YOU ARE IN CONTROL.

To begin your journey into progressive relaxation choose a quiet room, free from distractions. A moderate temperature is also important because it is difficult to relax when sweltering or shivering. Select a comfortable but firm chair. As in the thought-stopping technique, pay careful attention to body signals. Staying aware of yourself will help you achieve the concentration you need to relax. Concentrate on relaxing one group of muscles at a time, beginning with the back of the neck. (You may want to buy a book about progressive relaxation for a more detailed description.)[4]

SELF-CONTROL OF PHYSICAL SENSATIONS

I call a technique that combines features of thought-stopping and relaxation "self-control of physical sensations," because it depends heavily on your exercising control over physiological reactions that create sensations. While the technique requires self-discipline, it simultaneously helps a person hone his or her self-discipline.[5]

You begin by thinking of a situation that causes you discomfort, anxiety, or tension, whether at work or home. Choose a situation with a limited time span for your first attempt at this technique. Visualize in your mind exactly how you felt when last placed in this situation. Develop a rich sensory image of your physical sensations at the time. Was your face tense or furrowed? How much tension was there in your neck, back, hands, feet, and chest? How rapid was your breathing? Was your mind preoccupied?

If you cannot remember your physical sensations, make note of this important fact. There are important behavioral clues to your performance that are escaping you.

Each time you encounter your stressful situation again, take these next three steps:

1. Pay close attention to your characteristic physical reactions. Notice if your breathing is shallow or deep, rapid or slow, regular or irregular. What happens to your breathing when you are excited or pressured? Ask the same questions about your level of muscular tension. Are your hands relaxed or tight? Are your toes curled or extended? What feelings are you experiencing in your stomach or abdomen? Observe yourself closely just as you did in progressive muscle relaxation.

2. Each time you observe yourself starting to tighten up in some part of your body or to shorten your breathing, tell yourself that you are in control. You can short-circuit this habitual tendency. Take a moment to distance yourself from the habit, and convince yourself you can bring it under conscious control.

3. As soon as you notice a pattern of physical tightness and decide to overcome it, consciously relax. Allow the various muscles in your body to soften and flow. Direct your eyes to remain soft and relaxed. Observe the length of time you can maintain conscious control over your physical sensations. Observe also how quickly you return to ingrained, habitual

stress responses. Lengthen the amount of time you are able to remain in a calmer bodily state. Watch the effect on your mental skills.

EVERYDAY METHODS OF RELAXATION

The stress reduction methods presented so far require considerable self-control and self-discipline. As an important supplement to these more formal methods of stress reduction, you can incorporate stress-reducing activities into your everyday life. Self-discipline is important here so that you don't slip into the pattern of not dealing constructively with stress. The self-disciplined person creates the time to deal with stress and avoids excuses.

The table on page 187 presents twenty suggestions for everyday relaxation. An important feature of everyday methods of relaxation is that many of them require only several minutes per day. Several are more time-consuming: Taking a vacation requires at least a weekend, and becoming well-organized may require six months of disciplined effort.

An important message of this chapter has been that self-discipline is an essential part of stress management. Next, I focus your attention on the contribution of self-discipline to conquering problems that are life's major stressors.

20 METHODS FOR EVERYDAY RELAXATION

1. Plan to have at least one, brief idle period every day.
2. Talk over problems with a friend.
3. Take a nap when facing heavy pressures.
4. Have a good laugh—it's a potent tension reducer.
5. Concentrate intensely on reading, a sport, or a hobby. (Concentration helps you capitalize on enjoyment of the task, which leads to tension reduction.)
6. Go to the movies.
7. Breathe deeply, and tell yourself you can cope with the situation between inhaling and exhaling.
8. Have a quiet place or retreat at home.
9. Visualize yourself in an unusually pleasant situation.
10. Take a leisurely vacation during which every moment is not programmed.
11. Finish something you have started, however small. Accomplishing almost anything reduces some stress.
12. Decrease consumption of coffee, caffeinated soft drinks, and alcoholic beverages. Drink fruit juice or water instead.
13. Stop to smell the flowers, make friends with a child, or play with a kitten or puppy once in awhile.
14. Smile at least 5 minutes every day.
15. Strive to do a good job, but not a perfect job.
16. Work with your hands, doing a pleasant task.
17. Hug one person you like each day.
18. Take a nice hot shower.
19. Take a walk around the block.
20. Organize your desk.

CHAPTER 10

OVERCOMING ADVERSITY

Self-discipline enables people to persevere in overcoming obstacles and setbacks that vanquish the less disciplined and less committed. When faced with adversity, the self-disciplined person rises to the challenge and often emerges stronger. He calls upon inner resources to find creative solutions to the challenges at hand. As editor of *Success* magazine, Scott DeGarmo observes: "Each of us has immense untapped resources within ourselves. At the right moment, these deep reservoirs of willpower and creativity are unleashed."[1]

My purpose in writing this chapter is to describe how various components of self-discipline can help you overcome adversity. The implication is not that overcoming adversity is only a matter of self-discipline. My position, however, is that many of the best-established ways of managing adversity include at least a dose of self-discipline.

TEST YOUR RESILIENCY

People differ considerably in their ability to bounce back from a setback. Some are remarkably resilient, while others seem to crumble when faced with minor disappointment and frustration. Most of us fall somewhere in between these two extremes. The questionnaire on page 190 gives you an opportunity to gauge your resiliency. Understanding your capacity for bouncing back sets the stage for enhancing your resiliency.

RECOVERY THROUGH POSITIVE THINKING

Great comebacks are fueled with large amounts of optimism and positive thinking (including positive self-talk). In contrast, failed comebacks are often fueled by pessimism and negative thinking. In a nutshell, the person who readily overcomes adversity exercises the self-discipline to think positively. The contribution of optimism and positive thinking to overcoming adversity is reflected in many cliches and aphorisms. But there is much truth behind the words:

"Don't give up."

"Keep trying."

"You can succeed if you try."

"This too will pass."

"Happiness is just around the corner."

(text continues on page 195)

PERSONAL RESILIENCY QUESTIONNAIRE

Answer each of the following statements with *Mostly Agree* or *Mostly Disagree* as it applies to yourself.

	Mostly Agree	Mostly Disagree
1. Winning is everything.	____	____
2. I'm basically a lucky person.	____	____
3. If I have a bad day at work (or school) it usually ruins my evening.	____	____
4. A team that finishes last for two consecutive years should quit the league.	____	____
5. I enjoy rainy days because they are always followed by sunshine.	____	____
6. If somebody hung up the phone on me, I would stay angry with that person for a long time.	____	____
7. If a car splashes me with mud, it only bothers me for a few minutes.	____	____
8. If I just keep trying, I will get my share of good breaks.	____	____
9. When there's a flu epidemic going around, I'm one of the first people to catch it.	____	____
10. If it weren't for a few bad breaks, I'd be much further along in my career.	____	____
11. There is no disgrace in losing.	____	____
12. I'm a generally self-confident person.	____	____
13. Finishing last beats not competing at all.	____	____
14. I like to take big chances.	____	____
15. I would feel humiliated if I lost one week's income on an investment.	____	____

questionnaire continues

	Mostly Agree	Mostly Disagree
16. I'd rather not invite somebody to a party if there was any chance the person would say no.	____	____
17. If I want to be a home run hitter, I know I will strike out once in a while.	____	____
18. I'm a sore loser.	____	____
19. After a vacation, I need a day to unwind before returning to work.	____	____
20. Every "no" I encounter is one step closer to a "yes."	____	____
21. I doubt I could stand the shame of being fired.	____	____
22. I would be crushed if somebody turned down my marriage proposal.	____	____
23. I dwell over past mistakes.	____	____
24. I recover very quickly from a cold.	____	____
25. I find many days very discouraging.	____	____
26. The prospects of being heavily in debt frighten me.	____	____
27. I find it easy to form new personal relationships.	____	____
28. I think it's a good idea to avoid high-risk jobs.	____	____
29. If I've had a bad weekend, I find it difficult to concentrate on my work on Monday.	____	____
30. It's difficult for me to be optimistic about my career.	____	____
31. I have experienced bitter defeats several times in my life.	____	____
32. I take insults very personally.	____	____

questionnaire continues

	Mostly Agree	Mostly Disagree
33. If I ran for political office and were defeated, I would be willing to run again.	___	___
34. Losing my keys can keep me upset for a week.	___	___
35. I've gotten to the point where I just don't care about most things.	___	___
36. The prospects of failing to accomplish something important makes me shudder.	___	___
37. The last time I was rejected for a job I wanted, it had no particular impact on me.	___	___
38. It would be better to collect unemployment insurance than to waste my time looking for a job during a recession.	___	___
39. I rarely worry about what happened to me yesterday.	___	___
40. It takes a lot to get me discouraged.	___	___
41. If two consecutive banks rejected my application for a personal loan, I would forget about borrowing money for the time being.	___	___
42. I want better than an even chance of success before I risk investing time in an activity.	___	___
43. I seek revenge if I've been voted down on any issue.	___	___
44. It's a wise person who knows when to give up.	___	___
45. Catastrophes reported in the news make it difficult for me to concentrate on my work.	___	___
46. If I lost a favorite pet, it would take me at least a year to fully recover.	___	___

questionnaire continues

	Mostly Agree	Mostly Disagree
47. I get more than my share of good breaks.	____	____
48. I hold a grudge for a long time.	____	____
49. Fate has been unkind to me.	____	____
50. I enjoy being the underdog once in a while.	____	____

Scoring and Interpretation

Give yourself one point for each answer that agrees with the following key. Your score is the sum of all your answers that agreed with the key.

Statement Number	Resilient Response	Statement Number	Resilient Response
1	Mostly Disagree	20	Mostly Agree
2	Mostly Agree	21	Mostly Disagree
3	Mostly Disagree	22	Mostly Disagree
4	Mostly Disagree	23	Mostly Disagree
5	Mostly Agree	24	Mostly Agree
6	Mostly Disagree	25	Mostly Disagree
7	Mostly Agree	26	Mostly Disagree
8	Mostly Agree	27	Mostly Agree
9	Mostly Disagree	28	Mostly Disagree
10	Mostly Disagree	29	Mostly Disagree
11	Mostly Agree	30	Mostly Disagree
12	Mostly Agree	31	Mostly Disagree
13	Mostly Agree	32	Mostly Disagree
14	Mostly Agree	33	Mostly Agree
15	Mostly Disagree	34	Mostly Disagree
16	Mostly Disagree	35	Mostly Disagree
17	Mostly Agree	36	Mostly Disagree
18	Mostly Disagree	37	Mostly Agree
19	Mostly Disagree	38	Mostly Disagree

questionnaire continues

Statement Number	Resilient Response	Statement Number	Resilient Response
39	Mostly Agree	45	Mostly Disagree
40	Mostly Agree	46	Mostly Disagree
41	Mostly Disagree	47	Mostly Agree
42	Mostly Disagree	48	Mostly Disagree
43	Mostly Disagree	49	Mostly Disagree
44	Mostly Disagree	50	Mostly Agree

Very Resilient

If your score is 41 or higher, you are remarkably effective in bouncing back from adversity. When things go poorly for you, it hurts, but not for long. People in the very resilient category are usually emotionally mature and enthusiastic. They exercise strong self-discipline in overcoming setbacks.

Moderately Resilient

If your score lies between 16 and 40, you are moderately resilient. For as many times that you are able to bounce back readily when faced with adversity, there are times when you are much slower. You probably exercise a moderate degree of self-discipline when attempting to overcome adversity.

Not Very Resilient

If your score is 10 points or lower, you are probably the type of individual who is bowled over rather easily by adversity, disappointment, and setback. You tend to take reversals too seriously and are slow to get back up on your feet once tripped. You may give up too easily despite the fact that if you held on just a little longer, you would have attained your goal. You need to exercise more self-discipline in finding ways to overcome adversity.

"Wishing will make it so."

"If you think you can, you can."

"Goals make dreams come true."

"Keep up your spirits."

"Believe in yourself when the going gets rough."

"Just knock on one more door and you'll make it."

In support of positive thinking, psychologist Martin Seligman believes that optimism allows the human spirit to come back after adversity.[2] Optimists perceive a setback as a specific situation, rather than as a pervasive trend, and they do not place themselves at fault. They bounce back easily because they are persistent. (Pessimists may be more accurate at assessing risk. Yet they are more likely to surrender when negative situations arise.) Self-discipline keeps optimists focused on recovery goals. The optimist whose business burns down, for example, might say, "We'll be back in operation in 60 days, for sure." A heavy focus on a goal, in turn, facilitates persistence.

Make an Optimistic Interpretation of Events

One tool used by optimists to energize a comeback is to make an optimistic interpretation of events that others interpret pessimistically. This requires your disciplining yourself to develop the right mental set. Some examples of optimistic interpretations of events are listed on page 196.

Visualize a Happy Outcome

Overcoming adversity is yet another opportunity to apply visualization to achieve your goal. Imagine yourself enjoying the successful outcome to an adverse circumstance you are facing. Carefully see, hear, smell, and taste victory. Wishing alone won't

OPTIMISTIC INTERPRETATION

Adverse Circumstance	*Possible Optimistic Interpretation*
You lose your job.	Here is an opportunity to find a job I really want or start a new career.
Your significant other leaves you.	As traumatic as being dumped might be, maybe I will finally find somebody who loves me.
The last twenty-five leads you pursued refused to buy.	Not to worry. In this business, you have to call on dozens of prospects to make one sale. I'm one step closer to a yes.
You injure a tendon while playing your favorite sport.	I dislike being injured but here is an opportunity to get more things done around the house and do more professional reading.
Your organizational unit loses money for the third month in a row.	The picture isn't pretty, but the size of our loss is steadily declining.

make it happen, but visualizing a positive conclusion will prompt you to use all your creative energy to make it come true.

Don't Wallow in Self-Pity

The resilient person wastes little time commiserating over an adverse event. A committed golfer who was badly hurt in an automobile accident refused to give in to despair. "I'm lucky to be here," he said. With a crushed arm and connecting muscles to his hand severed, his chances of swinging a golf club again appeared small. But he did not give up hope. After several operations and seven months of intensive physical therapy, he returned to the golf course despite wearing a brace. His game is not as sharp as it was previously, but instead of wallowing in self-pity, he is thankful for the fact that he can still play golf.

BOUNCING BACK THROUGH PERSISTENCE

Persistence is the *sine qua non* of self-discipline. The self-disciplined person relentlessly persists in pursuit of a goal to which she is committed. Patience is an important component of persistence. The self-disciplined person accepts the fact that positive results may take a long time to achieve. A self-disciplined businessperson whose setback is a sullied reputation will fight long and hard to rebuild it. A self-disciplined individual abandoned by a spouse will patiently work through lead after lead to find a suitable partner.

A self-disciplined person is willing to invest as much time as necessary to achieve an important goal. (A person with limited self-discipline resents spending time in the pursuit of goals.) Despite their patience, self-disciplined achievers recognize when to cut their losses by changing goals. When the goals you have established fit neither the reality of the outside world, nor your own capabilities, it is time to change goals.

Hal, a middle manager laid off by a large electronics firm, persisted in looking for a comparable job in a similar firm. Two months into his job search, Hal recognized that similar firms were also reducing managerial layers. As a result, he changed his career position objective to becoming a member of a consulting firm or joining a small company. Two more months of job hunting resulted in a position as operations manager at an envelope manufacturer. The pay was lower than in to his former position, but he now had more authority.

The self-disciplined person also knows when persistence becomes an annoyance. For instance, Hal was told several times by a company not to contact them again. The signal was clear to him—he had to invest his energy elsewhere.

TRANSFORMING CHAOS INTO ORDER

Based on years of study, psychologist Mihaly Csikszentmihalyi concludes that resilient people are good at transforming chaos into order.[3] They are able to take a seemingly hopeless situation and convert it into an activity they can control and enjoy. Chaos spurs the self-disciplined person to new heights of imaginative problem solving. Entrepreneur Bal Dixit is an example of a person who transformed chaos into order to enable him to bounce back from severe adversity.

> **THE SELF-DISCIPLINED PERSON RELENTLESSLY PERSISTS IN PURSUIT OF A GOAL TO WHICH HE OR SHE IS COMMITTED.**

A native of India, Bal Dixit emigrated to the United States in 1964, and founded his company, Newtex, in 1978. He struggled for two years to establish a market for his product—fireproofing material for industrial products—and build a factory. Newtex then suffered a fire two days before the annual stockholders' meeting.

Bal vividly recalls seeing smoke billowing from the roof of his factory. When the doors were opened, oxygen fed the flames, creating an extremely dangerous situation. Although the company had fire insurance, thoughts raced through Bal's mind about the loss of customer confidence, employee morale, and a canceled stockholders' meeting.

Dixit's immediate reaction was to get everyone out of the building. While his office called the fire department, Bal sprayed the fire with an extinguisher, but the fire raged out of control. The television news teams were at the scene of the fire along with the fire department. Bal wanted to get control of the information communicated to the press, and he wanted to divert a panic by employees and business associates.

As soon as the fire was under control, Bal called all the employees together to discuss this major setback. His goal was to provide leadership and an optimistic attitude for his employees to follow. Bal told them that if they pitched in to help, he would guarantee their job security. Every employee present was given an emergency assignment and told not to discuss the fire with anyone. Dixit would field all questions from customers and the media. The employees worked day and night to clean up the soot and damaged equipment.

Every bit of damage was carefully documented with the total cost accounted for in detail. Dixit made the quick decision to go ahead with repairs before the insurance claims were covered, so that the company would not lose valuable time. Contractors were called in immediately to repair the roof and the treatment tower in which the fire started. The roof was repaired that weekend and within two weeks the tower was back in operation.

When the stockholders walked into the factory two days later, they knew about the fire but could not tell the true extent of the damage. Although Dixit thinks that his attention to the fire diverted some of his marketing efforts, Newtex met its sales forecast for the quarter. Since that time the company has continued to grow, and even performed well during the business slowdown of the early 1990s. Bal Dixit has received a New York State award for excellence in small business.

It would be hard to deny that much of the future of his company was ensured by Dixit's ability to make order out of the chaos of the fire. Employees still refer to that night as the "Dixit Fixit."

Three main actions and behaviors appear to be embedded in converting chaos into order. All of these actions provide suggestions for helping you use self-discipline to fashion a comeback.[4]

1. *Self-assurance without being self-conscious.* People who bounce back effectively believe strongly that their destiny is in their hands. Resilient people do not doubt that their own resources would be sufficient to allow them to determine

their fate. Dixit believed, for example, that he could regain control of his company. Although resilient people are self-assured they are not self-centered. Their energy is typically not directed toward dominating their environment as much as on finding a way to function within it harmoniously.

Tom, a 60-year-old electronic engineer, was laid off after thrity-five years of faithful service to one employer. Although he could eke out a living from his severance benefits and the company pension, he wanted more out of the rest of his career. Recognizing that he could not change the external world to make employers want to hire a 60-year-old engineer, Tom pursued a different track. He decided to become an as-needed contract engineer for small firms with small, or nonexistent, engineering staffs.

Tom systematically called on every small manufacturer in his region, offering to provide electronic engineering services on overload projects, at well below the market rate. Within four months, he was averaging 30 hours per week of professional work. As he put it, "I'm happier than ever. I'm sharing my expertise with loads of wonderful small business owners."

2. *Focus attention on the world.* People who transform adversity and its accompanying stress into enjoyable challenges do not spend much time thinking about themselves. They don't expend most of their energy attempting to satisfy their needs, or worrying about personal desires. Instead, they constantly process information about and from their environment, and so are able to adapt. Tom, the engineer, quickly recognized that the strongest demand for his services might be with small companies who could use his big-company expertise.

The focus for the self-disciplined person is still set by his goal. Yet he is mentally open enough to adapt to external events. By being open he is aware of alternative possibilities and feels a part of the surrounding world. The person who bounces back from a traumatizing injury processes the emotional shock and then seeks alternative ways of satisfying past interests. An avid tennis player who lost one leg in a motorcycle accident did not bemoan her fate for long. Instead she wore a prosthesis, played doubles instead of singles, and played with "C" instead of "A" players. She was so good at this level that she was more in demand as a player than ever.

3. *The discovery of new solutions.* When faced with psychic entropy, or chaos in the mental system, you face two paths. One path is to focus attention on the barriers keeping you from achieving your goals and removing them—by so doing, you restore harmony in consciousness. The second path is to size up the entire situation, including your own needs and desires, and investigate whether alternative goals might also be appropriate. In this way, new solutions to the problem caused by the adversity are possible. Tom's decision not to pursue corporate employment hints at this approach.

When people take themselves, their needs, and their desires too seriously, they're going to be in trouble as soon as things don't go their way. According to Csikszentmihalyi, they will not have enough disposable attention available to search for realistic options. Instead they will be surrounded by uncomfortable threats.[5]

To make the transformations from stressful adversity to joyful experiences, you must be prepared to perceive unexpected opportunities. Consider an executive living in San Francisco who lost her job in a political struggle. After conducting a nine-month job search, Denise couldn't find a position that supported her lifestyle. Angry and disappointed, she felt her world was crumbling.

If Denise had questioned why her lifestyle was so important, she would have opened new options. She could have sold her large house and moved into a smaller one, freeing herself to accept interesting employment that paid half as much as her previous position. By overcoming her mental set that a luxury lifestyle should not be modified downward, she could have opened new opportunities.

TAKING OWNERSHIP OF THE PROBLEM

Studies of the reactions of crisis victims provide useful clues to the nature of resilient people. People who accepted some responsibility for their experiences coped better than those people who blamed all of their misfortune on others.[6] Notice the similarity of this behavior to the self-discipline component of "minimize excuse making."

Self-blame when carried to extremes can be harmful. However, victims who accept some responsibility for a crisis may also have a feeling of control. Self-blame helped victims cope by giving them the opportunity to modify their behavior in such a way that would help them avoid becoming a victim in the future. A person who experiences the adversity of personal bankruptcy can rightfully blame easy credit and cultural pressures to consume as part of the problem. Yet to avoid similar financial troubles in the future, the person must admit to financial mismanagement.

Accepting some responsibility for adverse circumstances also reduces a sense of vulnerability. If you can exert at least partial control over what happens to you, it is possible to ward off some adversity. Because you feel you own the problem, you are more likely to do something about it.

FOCUSING ON SIGNALS OF GOOD NEWS

A curious, almost mystical, way of bouncing back from emotional hurt associated with adversity is to receive telltale signals from the outside world. The right signals will provide you a burst of optimism that can help ward off the depressive elements of adversity. Self-discipline is required to scan your environment and be alert to signals of good news. Once they appear, you can face others with renewed confidence and realize that good news is imminent.

Just as a bird's chirping signals the end of a heavy rainstorm, work and home offer their own signals of good times ahead. Not everybody gets the same signals, but here are a few that meant the turning point for some people:

- Sue was looking for a new relationship and she unexpectedly received an invitation to a house party.
- The federal tax bureau informed Michael in a letter that they recalculated his tax return. He and his tax advisor had erred in favor of the tax bureau; therefore, a check for $612.68 was enclosed.
- James noticed that a troublesome bald spot had grown in although he had not given it special treatment.
- Maureen had been trying to get an appointment for two weeks with a key executive at a company where she wanted to work. One morning his assistant phoned and said, "Mr. Sanchez will be able to see you at 11:30 tomorrow."
- A manager whom Barry insulted in a meeting last week smiled at him with forgiveness and invited him to join her for lunch.

- A five-year-old nephew hugged his aunt, and said "I love you" for the first time.
- A prospective customer of a large account returned Paul's phone call, asking to learn more about his company's product.

SELF-ASSESSMENT FOR CAREER RESILIENCE

A reality of the new workplace is that job security with one employer is less certain than ever. The informal, unwritten employment contract of the past was that companies such as GE, IBM, and GM would offer workers lifetime employment in exchange for adequate performance and some display of loyalty. Today's informal employment contract is that in exchange for high performance and a reasonable display of loyalty, the company will employ you for as long as you are needed. When your constellation of skills and job knowledge are no longer needed, you are walked out the door.

An increasing number of managers and professionals see themselves as freelancers who move from employer to employer as needed. Instead of being inveterate job hoppers, these mobile workers are merely responding to the reality of the job market.

In recognition of the realities of the new workplace, a *Harvard Business Review* report recommends that workers develop career resilience.[7] The career resilient workforce is composed of a self-disciplined group of employees who are dedicated to the idea of continuous learning. They also stand ready to reinvent themselves to keep pace with change and take responsibility for managing their own careers. At the same time they are committed to their company's success. The mental set of the career resilient workforce is similar to that of temporary workers and management consultants. Even though their relationship with each employer may be short term, they strive for high performance in each assignment.

The message for you is that you must develop a proactive response to the "clauses" of the new employment contract. A starting point would be to conduct a careful self-assessment of where your skills fit in with your current company or from a company from whom you may seek employment. Self-knowledge is essential to career resilience. You need to systematically take stock of the environments that bring out your best, the interests that ignite your motivation, and the skills that help you excel. You also need to choose an employer where you can make the greatest contribution. Know how your personal style affects others and in which environment you can function with maximum effectiveness. The following case history illustrates a successful application of self-assessment to prevent a career crisis.

Frank Aragona worked as a specialist in the customer service department of a plant that manufactures heating cables. After eight years of working in the same department, Frank thought he had reached a dead end. He believed he had learned all he was going to learn and had reached a plateau with the company. He faced two choices: leave the company or stagnate.

Aragona mustered his self-discipline to begin attending lunchtime seminars at a career center. By reading about careers in the center's library and working with a counselor on self-assessment, Aragona confirmed a long-felt desire to engage in new and different work. He also realized that some of his career interests, such as becoming a historian, were unrealistic at this stage of his life. "The center gave me a shot at reality and put things in perspective," he explains.

Armed with improved self-insight, Aragona's interest piqued when a coworker informed him of an opening in the international sales division. The job would capitalize on his customer service skills yet offer new challenges, including the excitement of international business. Aragona interviewed for the position and received an offer, along with a promotion and a raise.

Achieving self-insight requires self-discipline. You must invest the time and energy into asking yourself tough questions, getting feedback from others, and quite often going through the rigors of psychological testing. The career-development exercise on page 207 will help sharpen your insights about your career direction and capabilities.

USING SELF-DISCIPLINE TO PREVENT ADVERSITY

Up to this point I have described the curative powers of self-discipline in overcoming adversity. Self-discipline also prevents adversity. With an optimum level of self-discipline many problems can be avoided, from bankruptcy, to drunken driving, accidents stemming from carelessness, being fired because of a temper tantrum, and being convicted of misappropriating company funds. If you can resist temptation and abide by the reality principle, you can stay out of trouble.

THE MESSAGE FOR THE INDIVIDUAL WITH RESPECT TO CAREER RESILIENCY IS THAT ONE MUST DEVELOP A PROACTIVE RESPONSE TO THE CLAUSES OF THE NEW EMPLOYMENT CONTRACT.

The reflections of Louis Germain, a former camp counselor, provide insight into how being self-disciplined early in life can help a person stay focused on a success path. Germain recounts:

One day when we were getting ready to pick our basketball team, we decided to split up some of the kids. We would then conduct an intrasquad game to get a better feel for the skills of the players. Later in the day a tall kid was walking toward the camp ground with a basketball. As he approached Todd (the other counselor)

CAREER-DEVELOPMENT INVENTORY

Allow as much time as needed to answer the following questions. To help you answer some of the questions more accurately, solicit the opinion of people who know you well. Date your completed inventory and put it away for safekeeping. Examine your answers in several years to see (1) how well you are doing in advancing your career, and (2) how much you have changed.

1. How would you describe yourself as a person?
2. What are you best at doing? Worst?
3. In what types of job settings have you performed the best? The worst?
4. What are your two biggest strengths or assets?
5. What are the two traits, characteristics, or behaviors that require the most improvement?
6. What are your two biggest accomplishments?
7. What would be the ideal job for you?
8. Why aren't you more rich and famous?
9. What career advice can you give yourself?
10. Describe two peak experiences in your life.
11. What are your five most important values? (The things or beliefs in life most important to you.)
12. What goals in work and personal life are you trying to achieve?
13. How would you like your obituary to read?

and me, he appeared even bigger. He came up to us and said, "I heard that the basketball team is being picked today."

We told the young man that the game was only for kids who lived in the English Village area. He said that's where he lived. We then told him he had to be fourteen or younger to play on this team. He said he was thirteen. We were skeptical until one of our kids ran up to us and said, "Hey, it's John-John. Don't worry, guys, he's alright."

The tall thirteen-year-old proved to be a dominating player. Todd and I were each eighteen, but he outclassed us in one-on-one games. With big John on our team we won every game, including the championship.

Todd and I approached John one day and told him that he had the potential to be a Division I college basketball player. We also told him that he had to stay out of trouble to make it to the top. He told us he wanted to become a professional basketball player and that friends would laugh when he told them of his dream.

Toward the end of the summer, he approached Todd and me and described a long talk he had with his mother. The outcome was that they just weren't going to be able to afford college. We told John that basketball would get him through college. For the next four years, John worked as hard in school as on the court. In the process, he lost many friends, many of whom were dealing drugs and couldn't understand why John would waste his time studying.

Today John is none other than John (The Man) Wallace, the Syracuse University basketball star who is headed for a pro ball career. He talked to us one day during a pregame warmup and thanked us for the advice we gave him several years back. He told us that he could have very easily gotten caught up in the fast life of alcohol, drugs, robbery, and dropping out of school. Instead, with the help of his mother, us, and his faith, he disciplined himself to achieve his goals.

The John Wallace story has been repeated many times, but it has implications for all of us. If we develop strong self-discipline early enough in our career and personal life we can prevent adversity and experience reaching joyful goals. John Wallace was able to capitalize upon his talent by effective use of self-discipline. Today he is a star athlete headed toward a lucrative career. Without self-discipline he might have become yet another teenager running from one adversity to another.

THE PATH TO ECSTASY & PEAK PERFORMANCE

The transformational power of self-discipline points toward an inescapable conclusion. Self-disciplined people have more fun and get more out of life. Their heavy involvement in work and play makes possible greater joy of accomplishment and longer-lasting moments of ecstasy. The self-disciplined product planner experiences an inner glow as the product he has toiled with for so long is successfully launched. The self-disciplined software developer experiences intense pride as her patiently developed computer program becomes the flagship of the information systems department. The self-disciplined cat fancier glows with pride as his carefully groomed Siamese wins the best of breed at a regional cat show. And the self-disciplined, patient lover participates in intensely enjoyable sex for both partners.

Self-disciplined people achieve ecstasy and peak performance because they experience flow, a total absorption in what they are doing at the time. They concentrate so fully that the task at hand is virtually their only reality of the moment. Self-disciplined people love the tasks they choose to perform. The investment of love brings many happy returns, including a joyful experience and outstanding performance.

The purpose of this final chapter is to integrate many of the thoughts on self-discipline by explaining how you can move toward achieving the flow experience—the true path to ecstasy, peak performance, and happiness.

ATTRIBUTES OF PEAK PERFORMERS

A starting point in understanding how to achieve the flow experience is to examine the attributes of peak performers—those characteristics typical of people who regularly experience flow. As you read these attributes,[1] observe that peak performers are almost indistinguishable from self-disciplined people in general, because peak performance is yet another magnificent by-product of self-discipline.

1. *A sense of mission.* Peak performers have a sense of mission. They strive for a broader purpose and motivate others with their mission. The mission of a powerful and wealthy person might seem more exciting, but people in modest positions also have impressive, motivational missions. I know a peak performing FedEx regional manager who inspires others with his mission of becoming the highest-performing FedEx region in North America.

2. *Concern about results and process.* Peak performers obviously want to achieve outstanding results, so they set high goals

211

consistent with their mission. Yet, they also care about how they achieve these outstanding results. The peak performer cares about minute details and shows an artist's concern for savoring every part of a project. The peak performer chirps as she puts together a dazzling report for the company. She enjoys every stage of the process.

3. *Mental and physical calmness.* Perhaps the most remarkable attribute of peak performers is their mental and physical calmness as they proceed with their work. While focusing on the task they love, they are at ease. Think for a moment of being at your absolute best in performing a task. Reflect on your calmness as you made a skillful turn while skiing, effortlessly refinished a table top, or joyfully retrieved exactly the information you needed from your database. You were probably so absorbed in the task that you experienced no distractions, no mental static.

4. *Great powers of concentration.* Mental and physical calmness enables the peak performer to do what is necessary to achieve peak performance—concentrate intently.

5. *Sensory acuity.* The mental and physical calmness also assists the peak performer in sensing and responding to important information in the environment. Sensory acuity includes all the senses mentioned in Chapter 1 in relation to forming a sensory-rich vision. Although the peak performer experiences total concentration, he or she still responds to important signals. For example, the peak performing sales representative will detect a prospect's facial expression that the time is not quite right to say, "I have the contract ready for you to sign." Instead she might say, "I think we should talk about any other concerns you have about committing yourself today."

6. *Result-oriented activity.* To achieve peak performance, a person must produce meaningful results. As obvious as this

statement may seem, think about all the people you know who work hard yet produce very little. Around the office these people conduct a lot of meetings, produce exquisite graphics on their computer, and talk impressively—yet useful output is hard to find. Around the house, people who are not result oriented are busily engaged in many projects and have difficulty reading because they are so preoccupied with household tasks. Yet their home is no cleaner or neater than most, and they rarely entertain. The peak performer focuses on meaningful goals.

7. *Course correction.* Just as a self-disciplined person in general knows when it is time to modify a goal, peak performers can sense when they are off course. The peak performer senses when he has strayed from the best path toward goal attainment and then redirects his activity. The ability to process feedback from the environment is an important part of knowing when you are off course. Rick Leasure is an extraordinarily successful real estate agent who operates his own firm. One year he was the highest-producing agent in the United States for *Better Homes and Gardens.*

When Leasure was getting started in the real estate business, like most people, he aimed for selling large, expensive real estate. After awhile he sensed that this was a difficult, if not unrealistic, path for a beginner in his early twenties. Leasure then corrected his course by selling low-priced real estate within the city limits. "I'd take on the $35,000 properties that hardly anybody else would bother with. I could turn over these properties quickly and then move on to the next deal." As Leasure's reputation for results grew, he upgraded the properties he represented. His agency now lists some of the poshest pieces of real estate in town.

8. *Self-management through self-mastery.* Peak performers practice self-leadership; they achieve the results they want without constant prodding from a supervisor. Performance specialist Charles Garfield summarizes this attribute, "Employees who look for direction every time they have to make a move are a hindrance to their organization and themselves. The rising stars are those individuals who can align their own missions with an organization's mission, keep their motivation refreshed by achievement, aim for results, and manage themselves."[2]

ACHIEVING THE FLOW EXPERIENCE

The flow experience is akin to "being in the zone" in athletics. When you are in the zone you are achieving peak performance largely because your concentration is so complete. When the flow occurs, things go just right. You feel alive and fully attentive to what you are doing. In flow, there is a sense of being lost in the action. The common features of flow experience are high challenge, clear goals, a focus on psychic energy and attention, and continuous feedback. There is also a loss of self-consciousness. If you are experiencing flow, you are not concerned with yourself at the moment. A person who experiences flow is well-motivated, whether or not status, prestige, or large amounts of money are associated with the job. The comments of science fiction writer Ray Bradbury about his work characterize the flow experience:

> If you are writing without zest, without gusto, without love, without fun, you are only half a writer. It means you are so busy keeping one eye on the commercial market or one eye peeled for the avant-garde coterie that you are not being yourself. You don't even know yourself. For the first thing a writer should be is—excited.[3]

Flow is experienced frequently by people involved in creative work and in athletics. A singer is often totally absorbed in his or her singing. A soccer player may receive total enjoyment from stiffening his neck then passing a ball downfield by allowing the ball to rebound from his forehead. With proper application you can find flow in endeavors outside of creative work and athletics. A purchasing agent can find flow in smoothly negotiating a supplier contract for her firm. A data-entry clerk can find flow as he transposes data from one source into the computer.

The feedback you receive from doing a task correctly serves as a signal that things are going well. As the golf player hits the ball squarely in the middle of the driver, there is an immediate sound (a delightful thud) indicating that things are going well. In addition, a pleasant vibration moves up the arm. As the truck driver maneuvers properly around a curve, he or she receives a road-hugging feeling up through the wheels, indicating that the turn has been executed properly. As you make a presentation to higher management, and all eyes and ears are focused on you, you know you are performing well.

THE COMMON FEATURES OF FLOW EXPERIENCE ARE HIGH CHALLENGE, CLEAR GOALS, A FOCUS ON PSYCHIC ENERGY AND ATTENTION, AND CONTINUOUS FEEDBACK.

Despite the importance of control and feedback, the person who is experiencing flow doesn't stop to think what is happening. It is as if you are an onlooker and the precise actions are taking place automatically. Your body is performing pleasing actions without much conscious control on your part. When you are totally absorbed in reading a book, you do not realize you are turning the pages—your fingers take over for you.

Considering the importance of flow, it is fortunate that guidelines have been formulated to help you achieve flow for most activities. The essential steps in the process are as follows:[4]

1. Set an overall goal and as many subgoals as realistically feasible.
2. Find ways of measuring progress in terms of the goals chosen.

3. Keep concentrating on what you are doing, and keep making finer and finer distinctions in the challenges involved in the activity.

4. Develop the skills necessary to capitalize on the opportunities available.

5. Keep increasing your investment of psychic energy if the activity becomes boring.

To illustrate how to achieve flow, I will use an example of an activity that bridges work and personal life: preparing the long form for federal taxes—yes, your taxes! First, you set goals and subgoals such as (a) dates for total completion, and completion dates for portions of the task, (b) accuracy goals, (c) dollar amounts of legitimate deductions sought, (d) process goals, such as using software to prepare your taxes or filing your taxes electronically, and (e) learning about recent tax legislation.

Second, you will need to measure progress in terms of your goals. The response you get from the federal government will tell you how well your analysis compares with theirs. (The federal tax bureau's conclusion about the amount of your taxes, and your allowable deductions is, of course, the ultimate truth.) You can easily monitor whether you achieved the dates you established as goals. You can measure your progress in using software by evaluating whether your results are sensible. (I know someone who used tax preparation software for the first time and found that the Internal Revenue Service owed him $6,000,045 on taxable income of $56,575. He then searched for his errors!)

Third: concentrate! Tax preparation lends itself to concentration because errors are so costly. Keep focusing your mind on taxes exclusively when involved in the task. If you start to daydream, say to yourself, "Stop. Get back on target." The challenges in an activity force concentration. Trying to understand the many nuances in the tax instructions should force you to concentrate.

Seek out rather than avoid the challenges of understanding in more depth how to prepare taxes. Learning more about the tax preparation software is another challenge that should foster concentration. Recognize that the tax code is extraordinarily complicated with challenges even for knowledgeable accountants.

Fourth, determine the skills you need to do the job. It has become increasingly difficult to file taxes, particularly if all your income does not stem from salary. You may have to learn about such subjects as amortization, capital gains, and educational credits.

Fifth, put more of yourself into the tax preparation activity should you feel yourself becoming too detached. For instance, you could think of deductions that are not listed in the tax instructions and validate their legitimacy by asking an authoritative source, such as the tax bureau.

Achieving flow contains an element of the conflict between the pleasure and reality principles. The person in search of immediate gratification would tend to give up quickly when learning a complex activity. In contrast, if you invest the time to patiently develop a high skill level, you have the opportunity to experience flow. Rarely, however, does a beginner have enough skill in a complex activity to know the joy of flow.

ACHIEVING MENTAL TOUGHNESS

Without the flow experience, you are unlikely to achieve peak performance. Yet the flow experience does not account for all of peak performance. Another conception of peak performance is *mental toughness*. Sports psychologist James E. Loehr developed the term to refer to the ability to call upon one's talents and skills on demand in any situation.[5]

When you are mentally tough, you are resilient and self-disciplined, and you can stand up to competitive pressures.

Mental toughness involves a physiological state of arousal that allows the mind and body to reach its potential, or an *ideal performance state*. As in the flow experience, when you reach this state you feel relaxed, energized, alert, and confident. You can also feel a high level of concentration.

To develop mental toughness you not only concentrate on the task, but you also lead a healthy lifestyle that facilitates handling competitive pressures. Loehr recommends five strategies and tactics for becoming mentally tough. You will need to exercise self-discipline to stay on track with these approaches.

1. *Get physical exercise.* Expose your body to exercise so demanding that it produces physical stress. Any form of exercise will do the job, including walking up and down stairs, jogging, vigorously trimming bushes, or playing volleyball.

2. *Develop good sleep habits.* Sleep is the best form of recovery from competitive pressures, so maintain regular sleep habits. It is best to go to sleep and wake up at the same time every day. Get seven or eight hours of rest and sleep per night. Include power naps as part of your sleep program, especially before accepting a challenge in which peak performance is desirable.

3. *Laugh frequently.* Laughter relaxes the body and relieves stress. Be resourceful in finding material to make you laugh. Watch comedians on television, read humorous books and newspaper columns, observe preschoolers at play, and make up your own jokes. Also look for humor in serious situations. Observe how many CEOs receive $1 million bonuses while support staff is denied a cost-of-living adjustment. Notice

how people who complain about crime return clothing to a store after they have used it once for a special occasion.

4. *Put on a good show.* Even when you are down emotionally, generate the positive feelings and external image of confidence. Display an upbeat mood. A psychological theory that's been around for more than eighty years says that you feel the way you act: Act happy and confident, and shortly you will feel happy and confident.

5. *Carefully monitor your eating.* Eat five or six small meals each day rather than the traditional progression of a small breakfast, followed by a medium-size lunch, then a large dinner. Eating five or six small meals, of course, means that you have to be a nonconformist. During a business lunch when your workmates are ordering sausage and ziti, ask for a small container of yogurt or a salad and wheat crackers. Complex carbohydrates such as whole grains, vegetables, and fruits offer the advantage of stabilizing your blood sugar and moods. Stable moods facilitate achieving consistently high performance. The office manic who is occasionally brilliant when working 15 hours at a stretch also experiences many productivity dips.

> SELF-DISCIPLINE GIVES YOU THE POWER TO TRANSFORM OTHERWISE ORDINARY EXPERIENCES INTO MOMENTS OF PLEASURE AND ENJOYMENT.

SELF-DISCIPLINE, ENJOYMENT, HAPPINESS, AND ECSTASY

When *Getting it Done* was in its planning stages, I shared some of my ideas with an acquaintance. Her reaction was that very few people would want to read about self-discipline because it implies self-punishment, self-flagellation, strictness, and denial of pleasure. From her perspective, to be self-disciplined is to be cold, impersonal, and obsessed with work. As she interprets the term, a self-disciplined person whips herself for any deviation from an unforgiving routine. The point of view I have been attempting to communicate is just the opposite. To be self-disciplined is to experience enjoyment, happiness, and ecstasy.

Visualize yourself sitting in an outdoor cafe with a friend, a person of low self-discipline. The temperature is 90 degrees Fahrenheit (32 degrees Celsius), and the relative humidity is 95 percent. You both order a bottle of Canadian ale. The server returns in 5 minutes with your drinks. Being a self-disciplined person you concentrate intently on the ale. You experience the cool sensation of ale going down your throat; you are aware of the fine scent of brew; you look fondly at the droplets that have accumulated on the bottle. For the moment, you are a happy person. You have had a magnificent taste experience, and you have found pleasure in the situation.

Your undisciplined friend, however, is less fortunate. Gulping down the ale, he hardly notices the brand, and does not focus on the elegant flavor of the brew. While drinking the ale, he is thinking about how blasted hot it is outside, and wishes that the cafe were an enclosed, air conditioned restaurant. Your friend did achieve a modicum of thirst quenching but did not experience enjoyment or contentment.

The contribution of self-discipline to happiness and enjoyment transcends the experience of a good drink in a restaurant, but the principle is the same. Self-discipline gives you the power to transform otherwise ordinary experiences into moments of pleasure and enjoyment. If you are able to focus intently on the small details of a situation, you can enjoy them better. One of the reasons you are focusing on these small details is that they are part of a larger fabric called your mission. If part of your mission is to have an enjoyable social life, a glass of cold ale (or any other beverage) is one small drop in your bucket of total pleasure.

Ecstasy is an extension of enjoyment—at a higher level. To be ecstatic is to fully attend to the moment and savor small details that might go unnoticed by others. Have you observed how computer buffs can be ecstatic about the features of a computer that others might just dismiss as so many "bells and whistles"? The computer buff achieves ecstasy because she focuses on small details and features that are of little consequence to the person less compassionate about computers. To a self-disciplined computer buff, even the manual accompanying software is pure joy.

Ecstasy is often associated with sex, as it should be because few areas in life offer as much opportunity for pleasure and enjoyment. Yet for many people, sexual activity has lost its pleasure-generating possibilities. Some people in the same monogamous relationship for many years complain that their sexual relations have drifted into a ceremonial activity. About once a week, after the alarm is set, comes the sex. Some people who practice serial monogamy, or have multiple sex partners, also find that sexual pleasure has diminished.

However, many people achieve sexual ecstasy all their lives. Part of their pleasure derives from the self-discipline of being able to concentrate fully on sex while having sex, and to continue to search for nuances, details, and variations of sexual practices. The same people have the self-discipline to keep their relationship alive by continuing to learn about their partner. The combination of intense attention to the sexual act and to the partner allows one to be a sexual gourmand—even with the same partner for life.

SELF-DISCIPLINE IS TRANSFORMING BECAUSE IT ENABLES YOU TO ACHIEVE GOALS IN LIFE THAT STRETCH YOUR CAPABILITY THAT OTHERWISE MIGHT HAVE ELUDED YOU.

Happiness is more complex than enjoyment because it involves more control over your inner states. A happy person is in control of his own fate, including his interpretation of events. You control your fate through self-discipline. You are in control if you practice the self-discipline model: formulate mission statement → develop role models → develop goals for each task → develop action plans to achieve goals → use visual and sensory stimulation → search for pleasure within the task → compartmentalize spheres of life → minimize excuse making.

Self-discipline also helps you control your interpretation of events. Many wealthy people are unhappy because they know people who earn more money than they do. Many researchers are unhappy because they know other researchers who get published in more prestigious journals. Many married people are unhappy because they know a married person who has a spouse that is more physically attractive, wittier, wealthier, kinder, younger, more athletic, healthier, or less depressed than their spouse.

Self-disciplined people are not happier because they are delusional. They are happier because they can control their mental processes to focus on what is good, valuable, lovable, pleasurable, and ecstasy-provoking in their environment. Scott, a friend of mine, is always so cheerful despite not having the usual status and material objects that one associates with happiness. One day I asked Scott what made him so happy. He replied, "I have a wife who loves me and whom I love. We have two great adult children, and our debts are modest." Scott has good insight and good mind control. He focuses intently on the best things in his life, and evaluates them absolutely not relatively.

The reason self-discipline can bring you enjoyment, ecstasy, and happiness is the same reason self-discipline has the transformational power to help you achieve other important ends in life. With self-discipline as your great internal motivator, you are able to concentrate on the task at hand, thus maximizing productivity, quality, and satisfaction. Self-discipline is transformational because it enables you to achieve goals in life that stretch your capability that otherwise might have eluded you. Knowing how to develop and implement self-discipline is one of the most important gifts you can give yourself. With self-discipline on your side, you can finally get it done.

N O T E S

CHAPTER 1

1. Steve Devore, "Self-Discipline," *Executive Excellence*, December 1990, p. 3.
2. Ibid.
3. Diane Goldner, "Michael Crichton: The Plot Thickens," *USA Weekend*, January 7–9, 1994, p. 6.
4. Reported in *The Selling Advantage*, January 1994, p. 2.
5. Harrison G. Gough and Kevin Lanning, "Predicting Grades in College from the California Psychological Inventory," *Educational and Psychological Measurement*, Spring 1986, pp. 205–213.
6. Alvin G. Burstein and Frank G. Lawlis, "Desirable Psychological Characteristics of Medical Students: A Convergent Approach," *Multivariate-Experimental-Clinical-Research*, September 1976, pp. 173–187.
7. John A. Byrne, "The McKinsey Mystique," *Business Week*, September 20, 1993, p. 67.
8. William Raspberry, "Winning Lotto and Overcoming Racism," *Washington Post* syndicated column, January 15, 1993.
9. Parts of this model are based on *The Neuropsychology of Self-Discipline*, tape cassette program produced by SyberVision Systems, Inc., Pleasanton, CA, 1988; Devore, "Self-Discipline," pp. 3–5.
10. "Donna Inc.," *Time*, December 21, 1992, p. 54; "Woman on the Verge," *Working Woman*, May 1993, p. 66; "Unsuit Yourself: Management Goes Informal," *Fortune*, September 20, 1993, pp. 118–119.
11. Ian R. Gellatly and John P. Meyer, "The Effects of Goal Difficulty on Physiological Arousal, Cognition, and Task Performance," *Journal of Applied Psychology*, October 1992, pp. 694–704.

CHAPTER 2

1. Sigmund Freud, *The Complete Introductory Lectures on Psychoanalysis*, Translated and edited by James Strachey (New York: W. W. Norton & Company, Inc., 1966); Charles G. Morris, *Psychology: An Introduction*, 6th ed. (Englewood Cliffs, New Jersey, 1988), pp. 459–461. The diagram of the reality and pleasure principles is adapted from Morris, p. 460.
2. Gail Buchalter, "I Won't Make the Same Mistake," *Parade Magazine*, August 8, 1993, p. 8.

CHAPTER 3

1. Based on information in "Procrastination Can Get in Your Way," *Personal Report for the Executive*, December 24, 1985, pp. 3–4; "When to Procrastinate and When to Get Going," *Working Smart*, March 1992, pp. 1–2.
2. Stuart Kamen, "Conquering the Procrastination Habit," *Success Workshop* (published by The Pryor Report), Vol. 1, No. 3, 1992, p. 1.
3. Donnah Canavan, "Fear of Success," in Rebecca C. Curtis, *Self-defeating Behaviors: Experimental Research, Clinical Impressions, and Practical Implications* (New York: Plenum Press, 1989), pp. 159–188.
4. Quoted in Kamen, "Conquering the Procrastination Habit," p. 1.
5. Theodore Kurtz, "Ten Reasons Why People Procrastinate," *Supervisory Management*, April 1990, pp. 1–2.
6. "When to Procrastinate," p. 1.
7. Dru Scott, *How to Put More Time in Your Life* (New York: New American Library, 1980), p. 113.
8. Several items on the list are from Scott, *How to Put More Time in Your Life*, p. 115.
9. Kamen, "Conquering the Procrastination Habit," p. 2.
10. Wayne W. Dyer, *Your Erroneous Zones* (New York: Avon, 1976), p. 190.
11. Scott, *How to Put More Time in Your Life*, pp. 117–118.
12. Michael Maran, "Program Yourself: Software for the Right Side of Your Brain," *Success*, October 1991, p. 58. (Software produced by Visionary Software, Portland, OR.)
13. "Program Yourself for Success," *Executive Strategies*, January 1992, p. 8.

CHAPTER 4

1. Charles R. McConnell, "Self-management: Your Key to Success as a Supervisor," *The Health Care Supervisor*, April 1991, p. 6.
2. Research cited in Chris P. Nick and Charles C. Manz, "Thought Self-leadership: The Influence of Self-talk and Mental Imagery on Performance," *Journal of Organizational Behavior*, Vol. 13, 1992, pp. 683–684.
3. Adapted and expanded from "Working to Change Old Habits," *Working Smart*, May 1992, p. 8.
4. Ibid.
5. Charles C. Manz, *Mastering Self-Leadership: Empowering Yourself for Personal Excellence* (Englewood Cliffs, NJ: Prentice Hall, 1992), pp. 43–65; Charles C. Manz and Henry P. Sims, Jr., "SuperLeadership: Beyond the Myth of Heroic Leadership," *Organizational Dynamics*, Spring 1991, p. 24.
6. Manz, *Mastering Self-Leadership*, p. 51.
7. Ibid., pp. 54–62.
8. Manz and Sims, "SuperLeadership," p. 24; Manz, *Mastering Self-Leadership*, pp. 23–25.
9. Manz, *Mastering Self-Leadership*, pp. 66–89.

CHAPTER 5

1. Craig Nathanson, "Are You a Total Quality Person?" *Quality Progress*, September 1993, pp. 117–119.
2. Oren Harari, "Ten Reasons Why TQM Doesn't Work," *Management Review*, January 1993, pp. 33–38; Harari, "The Eleventh Reason Why TQM Doesn't Work," *Management Review*, May 1993, pp. 31, 34–36.
3. Oren Harari, "Three Very Difficult Steps to Total Quality," *Management Review*, April 1993, pp. 42–43.
4. Philip B. Crosby, *Quality Is Free* (New York: McGraw-Hill, 1979), pp. 200–201.
5. Thomas Teal, "Service Comes First: An Interview with USA's Robert F. McDermott," *Harvard Business Review*, September-October 1991, p. 117.
6. Donna Deeprose, "Helping Employees Handle Difficult Customers," *Supervisory Management*, September 1991, p. 6.

CHAPTER 6

1. Errol R. Korn and Karen Johnson, *Visualization: The Uses of Imagery in the Health Professions* (Homewood, IL: Dow Jones-Irwin, 1983), p. 132.
2. Alan J. Rowe and James D. Boulgarides, *Managerial Decision Making: A Guide to Successful Business Decisions* (New York: Macmillan Publishing Company, 1992), p. 172.
3. Quoted in "Breakthrough Ideas," *Success*, October 1987, p. 50.
4. Bryan W. Mattimore, "Breakthroughs," *Success*, November 1988, p. 46.
5. This section is based on Bryan W. Mattimore, *99% Inspiration: Tips, Tales & Techniques for Liberating Your Business Creativity* (New York: AMACOM, 1993), pp. 118–119.
6. Ibid., p. 127.
7. Mattimore, "Breakthroughs," p. 46.
8. Mattimore, *99% Inspiration*, pp. 83–87.

CHAPTER 7

1. This section is based on Daniel Araoz, "Thinking for Success," *Executive Management Forum*, October 1990, p. 4.
2. The model presented here is based on Thomas V. Bonoma and Gerald Zaltman, *Psychology for Management* (Boston: Kent Publishing Company, 1981), pp. 88–92.
3. William Raspberry, "Laziness Is Killing Writing and Jazz," *Washington Post* syndicated column, June 23, 1994.
4. Scott DeGarmo, "Great Comebacks: Despite It All, They Triumphed," *Success*, July/August 1994, pp. 4, 31.
5. Based on Charles G. Morris, *Psychology: An Introduction*, 6th ed. (Englewood Cliffs, NJ: Prentice Hall, 1988), p. 249.
6. Chris Argyris, "Teaching Smart People How to Learn," *Harvard Business Review*, May-June 1991, pp. 99–109.

7. Robert E. Kaplan, Wilfred H. Drath, and Joan R. Kofodimos, "High Hurdles: The Challenge of Executive Self-Development," *The Academy of Management Executive*, August 1987, p. 195.
8. Evan I. Schwartz, "Interrupt-Driven," *Wired*, June 1994, p. 46.
9. Allen C. Bluedorn, Carol Felker Kaufman, and Paul M. Lane, "How Many Things Do You Like To Do at Once? An Introduction to Monochronic and Polychronic Time," *The Executive*, November 1992, pp. 17–26.
10. Carol Felker Kaufman, Paul M. Lane, and Jay Lindquist, "Exploring More Than 24 Hours a Day: A Preliminary Investigation of Polychronic Time Use," *Journal of Consumer Research*, Vol. 18, 1991, pp. 392–402.

CHAPTER **8**

1. Quoted by Jeffrey Lynn Speller, *Executives in Crisis* (New York: John Wiley, 1989), p. 4.
2. Michael E. Cavanagh, "Myths Surrounding Alcoholism," *Personnel Journal*, February 1990, p. 112.
3. Based on Harriet B. Braiker, "What All Career Women Need to Know About Drinking," *Working Woman*, August 1989, p. 72.
4. David L. Watson and Roland G. Tharp, *Self-Directed Behavior: Self-Modification for Personal Adjustment*, 2nd ed. (Monterey, CA: Brooks/Cole Publishing, 1977), p. 15; Gary P. Latham and Colette A. Frayne, "Self-Management Training for Increasing Job Attendance: A Follow-Up and a Replication," *Journal of Applied Psychology*, June 1989, p. 412.
5. Watson and Tharp, *Self-Directed Behavior*, p. 39.
6. Ibid., pp. 114–115.
7. Patti Singer, "Losing & Winning," *Rochester New York Democrat and Chronicle*, May 24, 1994, pp. 1C, 6C; Personal interview with Angela Vitello, July 1994.

CHAPTER **9**

1. Robert L. Campbell, Lawrence W. Svenson, and George K. Jarvis, "Perceived Level of Stress Among University Undergraduate Students," *Perceptual and Motor Skills*, October 1992, pp. 552–554.
2. Philip L. Rice, *Stress and Health: Principles and Practice for Coping and Wellness* (Monterey, CA: Brooks/Cole Publishing, 1987), p. 306.
3. Midge Wilson, "First Aid for Stress," *Success*, September 1982, p. 13.
4. An excellent description of progressive relaxation is found in Rice, *Stress and Health*, pp. 237–255.
5. Ingrid Lorch-Bacci, "High Impact Exercise," *Executive Management Forum*, January 1991, p. 4.

CHAPTER **10**

1. Scott DeGarmo, "Rebounding: Learn the Art and Discipline of Bouncing Back," *Success*, July/August 1993, p. 4.

2. Duncan Maxwell Anderson, "Learn to Bounce Back," *Success*, July/August 1994, p. 41.

3. Mihaly Csikszentmihalyi, *Flow: The Psychology of Optimal Experience* (New York: Harper Perennial, 1990), pp. 201–208.

4. Csikzentmihalyi, *Flow*, pp. 203–208.

5. Ibid., p. 207

6. Julius Segal, *Winning Life's Toughest Battles: Roots of Human Resilience* (New York: Ivy Books/Ballantine, 1986), p. 64.

7. This section, including the case history, is based on Robert A. Waterman, Jr., Judith A. Waterman, and Betsy A. Collard, "Toward a Career Resilient Workforce," *Harvard Business Review*, July-August 1994, pp. 87–95.

CHAPTER 11

1. Charles Garfield, *Peak Performers: The New Heroes of American Business* (New York: Avon Books, 1987), pp. 22–52; Ingrid Lorch-Bacci, "Executive Management Forum," January 1991, pp. 1–4; Michael Rozek, "Can You Spot a Peak Performer?" *Personnel Journal*, June 1991, pp. 77–78.

2. Garfield, *Peak Performers*, p. 40.

3. Quoted in Joan Crowder, "Prolific Ray Bradbury Busy Teaching Enthusiasm," *The New York Times*, syndicated story, March 8, 1990.

4. Mihaly Csikszentmihalyi, *Flow: The Psychology of Optimal Experience* (New York: Harper Perennial, 1990), p. 97.

5. Based on and adapted from James E. Loehr, "You Can Do It, Too," *USA Weekend*, July 15–17, 1994, pp. 5–6.

INDEX

229